Alec French Architects

Thirty years of practice 1980-2010

RICHARD LEE and DAVID MELLOR

First published in 2011 by Alec French Architects
27 Trenchard St, Bristol, BS1 5AN, UK
T: 0117 929 3011
www.alecfrench.co.uk

© Richard Lee, David Mellor
ISBN: 978-0-9568016-0-9

British Library Cataloguing-in-Publication Data
A catalogue record for this book is available from the British Library
Designed by Stephen Morris: smc@freeuk.com   www.stephen-morris.co.uk

Cover image: Marketing and Exhibition Centre, Bristol. Photo: Roger Ball

Printed in the Czech Republic via Akcent Media

Contents

Foreword

This book records the work of Alec French Architects, previously Alec French Partnership, over the thirty years from 1980-2010.

The practice, established by Alec French in the late 1920s, was headed by Michael Collings and Ian Thornton when Richard Lee joined in 1977, followed by David Mellor in 1979. Richard Silverman, who moved on to become professor of architecture and head of school at Cardiff University, was also a director from 1985-87.

We acknowledge Michael and Ian's great contribution to the strengths and reputation of the practice.

Nigel Dyke and Mark Osborne became Directors in 2002 having previously played key roles in the practice. The central section of this book illustrates projects representative of this period under the leadership of Richard and David and discusses their approach to the Art of Architecture. A further section introduces work that Nigel and Mark have directly led, adding their own expertise and distinctiveness, but also continuing to explore the themes discussed in this book.

Architecture is very much a team activity and we have very much appreciated and benefited from the contributions made by all those who have worked with us over the thirty years.

We also acknowledge the key roles played by other members of the design team. Good buildings benefit significantly from the input and expertise of structural and services engineers and good cost advice is critical, particularly at the early stages. The best buildings are also dependant on good contractors and the knowledge and input of specialist suppliers.

None of this work would be possible without our clients. We have been fortunate to work with some of the best who have engaged with the design and building processes and who value good design.

We would also like to express our thanks to the creativity and patience of our designer, Stephen Morris, and to the calm dedication of Sharon Fennell in revising texts and sourcing images. We have also much appreciated the support of our wives and families over this endeavour.

Richard Lee, David Mellor
March 2011

Setting the Bristol Scene Richard Lee

The Bristol scene in the late 1970's when I joined Michael Collings and Ian Thornton at Alec French Partnership was full of challenging opportunities for architects. I had visited the city in the autumn of 1967 with my wife for the first time and we decided instantly that this was the place to put down roots. Within three years I had formed a small practice in Berkeley Crescent where we flourished on a programme of small works and part-time teaching.

During this period I, like other local architects, became very concerned at the environmental implications of the 1966 Development Plan Review, especially the ruthless highways planning and the zoned approach to uses.

Ring roads as proposed, 1966

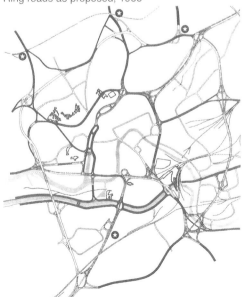

Furthermore I believed that this beautiful city deserved better new architecture that was respectful of its great legacy of Georgian and Victorian buildings. Despite the post war period of reconstruction and change, Bristol still retained much of its character unlike, say Plymouth, where new post-war masterplanning had swept away most remnants of the old city's historic charm and complexity. In Bristol a brief look at the 1880's Ordnance Survey maps tells you that many of the inner suburbs of the city remain, to this day, largely intact.

In 1967 the city docks faced closure to commercial shipping and moved down-stream to Avonmouth, leaving some 175 acres of disused industrial land with over three miles of water frontage in the heart of the city. To some this offered an opportunity to reclaim land by infilling the docks for new commercial development, but others could see a unique opportunity for the city fathers to call for a vision of a mixed living, working and leisure city, and the end of zoned city planning.

Groups such as the City Docks Group (1973) and the Bristol Civic Society put pressure on the city council to exploit the special character of Bristol which, to many of us, had the potential to be compared with great European cities such as Amsterdam and Venice.

The battles that were fought to save Bristol's heritage were at their height in the 1970's. People expressed their differences in Public Inquiries and became well organised, successfully fighting inappropriate proposals such as the Outer Circuit Road. Building on this spirit and with the help of others including John Grimshaw and Adrian and Sue Jones, we organised exhibitions in 1975 and 1976 under the banner of 'Twenty Ideas for Bristol' which enjoyed support and contributions from local people about their city.

Twenty Ideas: Queens Road proposal

Francis Greenacre of the City Council backed the initiative and made the City Museum and Art Gallery available, thus encouraging a new rapport between public and private interests and giving voice to environmental and community issues.

The *Architects Journal* described the experience aptly: 'To enter the exhibition from the world outside is to exchange the dreary pessimism of 1975 Britain for a joyous optimism allied to creative design and social responsibility.'

In 1975 I met Michael Collings in Moscow on an architectural visit and in 1977 I accepted an offer of partnership from Alec French Partnership, a thriving Bristol-based firm of architects with roots back to the 1920s. I took this decision on the basis that no significant commissions would come our way as a small practice and to help change Bristol's new architecture for the better one would need an influential vehicle such as Alec French Partnership.

Working with the architect-led Urban Design Section in the City Council planning office, local architects, including ourselves, began to develop a new architectural 'characterisation' of the city. For example buildings such as the WCA and Buchanan's warehouses on Redcliffe Backs characterised the Floating Harbour by building sheer off the dock wall and, where possible, providing pedestrian access through at

quay level. Others used polychromatic brickwork and rubble stone. This approach supported the policies of the new Conservation Areas spreading across the city and encouraged greater liaison between architects, artists and craftsmen.

By 1978 the considerable number of new brick buildings in the city centre heralded the end of an era of concrete clad buildings, which, to the public, were usually considered 'inhuman, huge and ugly' (*The Fight for Bristol*, Priest and Cobb). The gulf between architects and their public thirty years ago was wide and had to be narrowed and more common ground found.

It was against this background of concern for the loss of historic buildings and a growing conservation and amenity society movement in the city, led by Jerry and Anne Hicks and Dorothy Brown to name but

three of the key players, that the practice took up the challenge of finding contemporary languages, respecting, where appropriate, Bristol's architectural legacy but without resorting to pastiche.

Our first opportunity to design a significant new building in brickwork was Broad Quay House for Standard Life, which was to replace the CWS building at the head of St Augustine's Reach. The CWS building was a familiar and popular landmark to Bristolians even though built in the robust vernacular of a red brick Manchester architecture not entirely appropriate for this Bristol waterside location.

The new building was designed in 1978 during the second oil crisis when there was a real nervousness that oil production would fall dramatically, energy costs rise

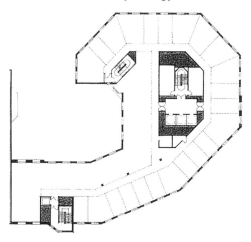

Broad Quay House plan

and deep plan energy consuming buildings become uneconomic. There was also the beginning of an awareness that oil reserves were finite.

The 'coiled' plan form of Broad Quay House was built around the boundaries of the site enabling opening windows to naturally cross-ventilate the offices, if required. It also, significantly, restored the edges of the surrounding streets.

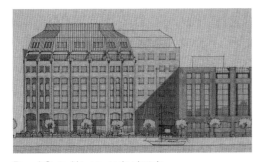

Broad Quay House, early sketch

The building design sought to recapture the massive characteristics of its predecessor using blue/red engineering brick and well recessed openings. The roof was intended to be in lead, hence the 'flying' rainwater chutes that visually anchor it, but a change of roof covering to slate at a late stage lost this integrity and was, in my view, regrettable.

Philippa Threlfall and Kennedy Collings designed 15 terracotta panels, integrated into the brickwork, depicting aspects of Bristol's history through eight centuries from

Terracotta panels, Broad Quay House

the City's Royal Charter in the thirteenth century to the building of Concorde. Standard Life also commissioned sculptor Gerald Laing to design a major bronze fountain in the centre of the courtyard of Broad Quay House, called the 'Apotheosis of Sabrina' after the Romano-British goddess who drowned herself in the River Severn and is reborn from the depths riding on a shell reminiscent of Botticelli's *Venus*. The experience of working with these artists increased our determination to involve artists and craftsmen in our buildings, whenever possible.

My contextual approach to architecture evolved out of a strong interest and respect for the genius loci of a site, through its archaeology, history and topography. I had also been impressed by the Land Use and Built Form research work of the Martin Centre at Cambridge in the late 1960's. This demonstrated the option of building low around the perimeter of a site and

achieving similar density to high-rise Corbusian towers.

We had the opportunity of putting this to the test at Brunel House and St Bartholomew's, Bristol, enabling us to knit new buildings into historic contexts without building uncomfortably high. This approach enabled us to create continuous streets and public spaces in contrast to many of the fragmented developments that had occurred across post war Britain.

In 1977, when I joined the practice, we had entered a new era with David Mellor joining us in 1979.

St Bartholomew's offices

New Challenges David Mellor

Richard and I had read architecture in the same year at Cambridge. After our diploma years he departed to set up his own practice in Bristol and I embarked on a PhD, under the excellent guidance of Michael Brawne, looking into how people perceive and respond to different types of spaces. Though I did not complete my doctorate, preferring to go into practice, this research undoubtedly increased my awareness of the interaction between people and places which has remained an integral part of my approach to design. As Aalto said

a truly functional architecture must be functional from a human point of view.

Whilst not a determinist, I do believe in an architecture that can enable a wide range of human responses.

A great pleasure over the years has been travelling to see work that I find sympathetic. Aalto's Saynatsalo town hall in the snow of October fitting like a warm glove; Viipuri Library not destroyed (if in need of attention); discovering De Carlo's wonderful interventions in Urbino and the delights of Van Eyck's Mothers Home. Hill House, the Robie House, the Villa Savoye, Ronchamp and the work of Glen Murcutt are others that come immediately to mind. The elegant manipulation of space, form, light and materials in these buildings, lifts the spirit, and restores one's confidence in the potential of a responsive architecture of our time.

In 1968 I joined the architects' department of the London Borough of Southwark. The inner London boroughs were at that time exploring innovative high density, medium rise, housing solutions – a different model to the towers and slabs of only a few years earlier. Rejecting Southwark's earlier system building and universal second floor

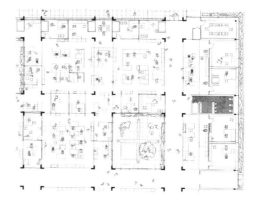

Lucas Industries HQ, plan and section

walkways, we chose to design in brick and to connect families to the ground.

Three years later Colin St J (Sandy) Wilson asked me to join his practice, initially working on the housing and other aspects of the Bloomsbury version of the new British Library. They were enjoyable and heady days in a great studio. Later I

worked closely with Sandy on a new Headquarters for Lucas Industries, won in a limited architecture competition. This was a geat opportunity to explore the concept of giving identity to working groups within a flexible and adaptable space, ideas explored by Sandy in his Liverpool Civic Centre scheme and also by Hertzberger in his Appeldoorn offices that I had been very impressed by on a visit some years earlier. Though sadly Lucas was not finally built, it has been credited as having made a major contribution to office design and it was to influence my work on the Aardman Headquarters many years later.

By the late 1970s though, after working on the Northampton City Hall competition and completing a sheltered housing scheme in Haringey, I was needing new challenges.

Although very happy living and working in London, it was not an easy financial climate in which to set up my own practice and we made the difficult decision to look for another compatible city. Bristol felt like a city in which we could enjoy living and become a part of.

I had taught for a few years at the Bristol School of Architecture, and my wife had done some field research in London for a cohort study based at the Department of Child Health at Bristol University. We had kept in touch with the Lee family over the years and joining Richard at the long

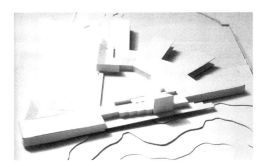

Northampton City Hall

established Alec French Partnership, with which he had recently merged his practice, clearly offered major opportunities to design and to build.

Alec French Partnership had a strong reputation for work well built and a strong professional ethos. The then Directors had, however, realised the need for new ideas and direction. I joined the practice in September 1979.

Over the 30 years of this book Bristol has become an increasingly lively and forward looking city to which we hope we have contributed.

Our Approach to Architecture

We have shared beliefs in the process of design and enjoy similar approaches. We enjoy working closely with our clients, helping to develop their briefs and understanding their aspirations. We strive to create an appropriate sense of place and ambience. We are very conscious of context and carefully consider the appropriate response.

Our shared Cambridge architectural education has given us our fundamental approaches to the Art of Architecture, enriched and developed over thirty years of practice together. From those student experiences we learnt the importance of having a clear rationale and the benefits, indeed the moral imperative, of making proposals with integrity and appropriateness. From Peter Eisenman, our first-year tutor, we learnt about the language of architecture and an understanding of principles of form, light, movement and legibility, albeit in an intentionally abstracted form. Colin St J (Sandy) Wilson, then a senior lecturer and key figure at the School, inspired us with a lively history of the Modern Movement. He showed us the range of inventive formal explorations of Le Corbusier and increasingly shared with us his enthusiasm for the 'other tradition' as exemplified by Aalto, Scharoun, Haering and others. He was also a great studio master.

It was noted by external critics that as a group of students our year showed little sign of direct influences from current architectural fashions, and our own work has not been driven by particular 'styles'. However that is not to deny the legacy of architecture that all good architects draw upon. Inspiration comes from hundreds of years of architecture, but today we also have over 100 years of the Modern Movement to learn from, to be inspired by, to understand the thinking behind it and to judge the qualities of the built spaces over time. A list of personal heroes would be headed by Aalto and Wright, but we enjoy and have been inspired by a wide range of work.

Our approach is very much in line with the position of Sandy Wilson as set out in his seminal book, *The Other Tradition of Modern Architecture: the uncompleted project*. He identifies architecture as a 'Practical Art which serves an end other than itself' – the end being defined as a rich interpretation of the brief, a response to place and forms and technologies that are appropriate. We also subscribe to the social consciousness and humanity of that tradition and we have always enjoyed the pleasures of working closely with the people we are building for and the wider communities our buildings relate to.

In the design process the plan and section remain for us key generators of form. Elevations and their material choices are then a product of the appropriate feel and expression of the building and the context.

We hope our architecture is expressive and responsive with a richness that comes from creative dialogue with our clients, a considered response to context and an awareness of the properties of materials. Our approach is pragmatic in that it responds to the particularities of brief and site, without imposing either a prescribed fixed geometry, or a preconception of 'style'. We do however strongly believe in there being clear reasons for doing things, ideally several overlapping good reasons.

Whilst dividing this brief essay into the constituents of Brief, Context, Sustainability and Urban Design, we are conscious of the holistic nature of the design process. We also recognise those aspects which are less easily articulated – responses that are emotional, often instinctive and based on personal experience, which also affect the form of the solution.

Well considered architecture enjoying the intrinsic nature of each project is always challenging, but the best results can be very rewarding.

Offices, Redcliff Quay Bristol 1991

Standard Life owned the Sand Wharf on Redcliff Backs in 1974 and then purchased the two adjoining warehouses in 1979 giving a frontage to the floating harbour of some 100 metres. Their brief was for a high quality office environment taking full advantage of this waterfront location.

The urban design brief from the city planners centred around the retention of the vista from King Street to the medieval tower of St Thomas the Martyr helping to tie Redcliffe into the city centre and opening up new pedestrian routes via a proposed footbridge across the Floating Harbour, as yet unbuilt.

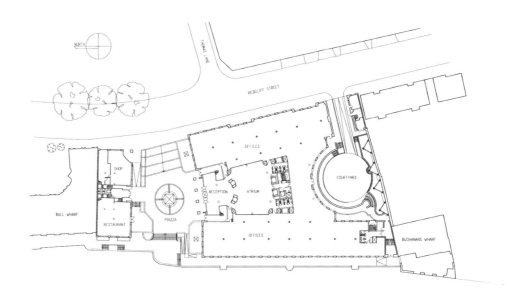

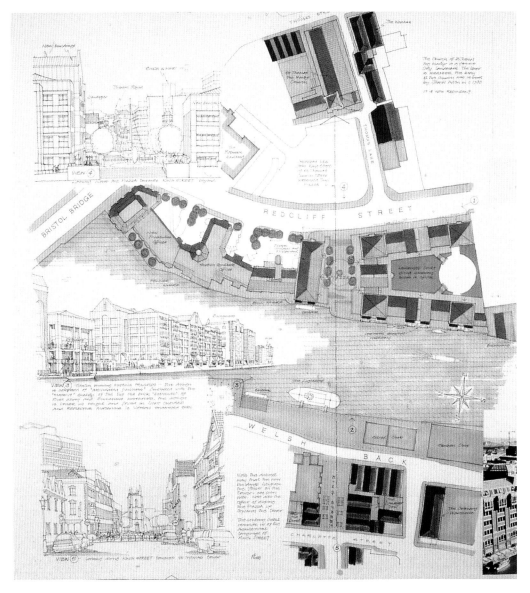

Our response was to recognise the essential characteristics of these derelict war-damaged warehouses which, as the remaining one to the south, rose sheer from the dock wall, were surmounted with parapets and suppressed slate roofs and contained projecting platforms and hoists to unload from ships. Our approach re-interprets the essence of that vernacular in its massing and forms; balconies and brise soleil replace loading platforms. These add to the layering of the elevations and give proportion and articulation better relating it to the incremental scale of Bristol's traditional quayside warehouses.

The initial proposal used cream and red stove enamelled rainscreen panels. The final design uses brick and stone whilst retaining much of the original design intention. This change followed a complicated planning history and much consultation about the architecture, materials and urban design in this important Conservation Area. The planning history is well documented by John Punter in his study *Design Control in Bristol 1940-1990*.

Drawing by David Hope, showing proposed footbridge

During design development the open court-yard became an enclosed 'atrium' with a glazed lantern and glass lifts.

Continuing the tradition in the Practice to engage with the history and archaeology of a site and to express this through public art, Standard Life commissioned Philippa Threlfall and Kennedy Collings (artists responsible for a number of ceramic works including the roundels at Broad Quay House) to design a centrepiece to the piazza. With James Blunt they created a ceramic obelisk capped by an armillary sphere locating the accurate latitude of the site and depicting the sea creatures that might be encountered at the 'end of the world'. The inspiration for these creatures came from early illustrations found in the Wells Cathedral library and the history of Redcliff Backs. The medieval quays had, in all probability, seen the embarkation of John Cabot onto his boat the *Matthew* in 1497 to discover Newfoundland.

Marketing and Exhibition Centre for Bristol Development Corporation 1993

The Development Corporation required an
exhibition space for the display of its
proposals for the regeneration of this part
of the city, in the context of Bristol and its
history. Coming to the building needed to
be an enjoyable and stimulating experience
for a range of visitors from local business-
men and school children, to politicians and
potential investors.

The building was required to:

*be innovative in design and to
demonstrate the Corporation's
commitment to high quality modern
design.*

It was to be relocatable after a few years to
another short-life location and expected to
have several locations in Bristol before
becoming a permanent community facility.
This design was the winner of a limited
regional competition. It was developed by
architect and engineer over a long

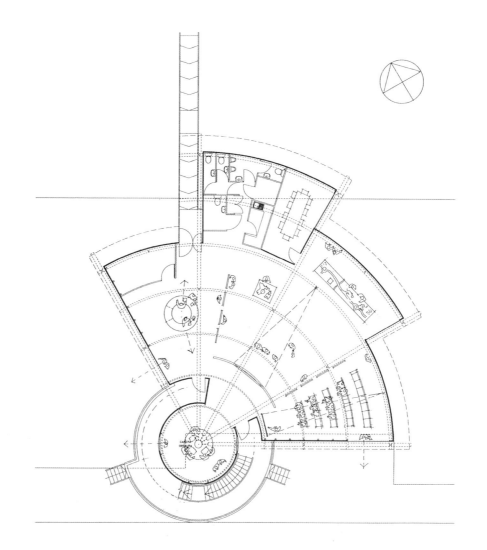

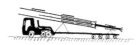

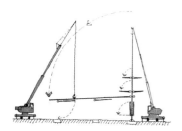

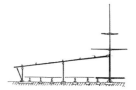

weekend and was, unusually, built almost exactly as the competition drawings.

The building was designed to attract attention both by its form, structure and materials, and by the quality and interest of the experience it offers to the visitor.

The design responds to the initial site, and likely future sites, from which there is no clear view at ground level of the areas being redeveloped. The visitor's experience therefore culminates in a seven-metre high viewing platform which dramatically opens up an awareness of the surroundings and an understanding of how future plans might relate to them. This is protected from the weather by a canvas canopy surrounding a smaller, higher 'crows nest' for more distant views. The potential is also offered for a late-twentieth-century version of a Victorian 'camera obscura' with a complex of mirrors replaced by a controllable video camera at the top of the mast. This would allow views over the Corporation's area and central Bristol, whilst at the same time allowing the superimposition of videos of future plans.

The open and flexible exhibition space is generated from the central mast and camera obscura drum, in a radiating form that accommodates entry from both land and water and provides a sequence of

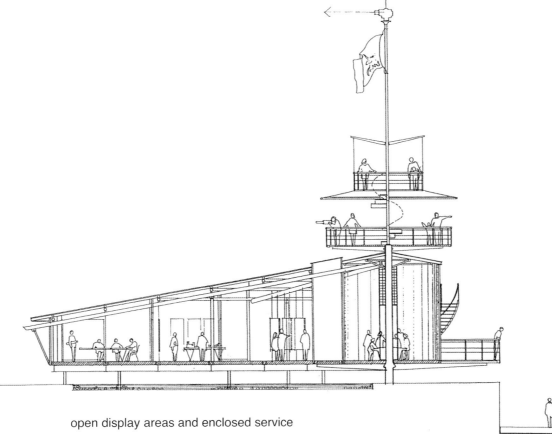

open display areas and enclosed service areas. The radiating structure is experienced internally and externally and is integrated with controllable natural and artificial lighting.

The mast is also key to the initial construction and subsequent re-erection of the building. The primary beams and columns arrived on site folded to the mast, thereby minimising site works and helping to achieve both the initial completion date and future relocation.

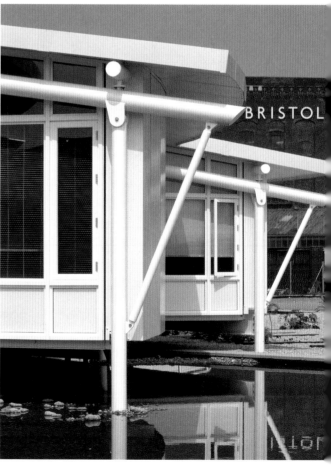

The external walls are composite steel panels and the roof and floor are of twin skinned plywood construction. All enclosing elements are demountable and reusable other than the single ply roofing membrane.

Composite panels were chosen for their inherent structural and insulating characteristics, and also provide the required demountability. The white panels give a sparkle and crispness appropriate to its function, context and scale.

The pool in which the building is set reflected the Corporation's aspirations for the use of water and helped the building establish its own context in what were then rather featureless surroundings.

The building was completed in 17 weeks. Once this site was needed for redevelopment the building was dismantled and is planned for re-erection as designed but outside Bristol.

Claire Palley Building St Anne's College Oxford 1992

In 1990 the practice was commissioned by St Anne's College Oxford to draw up options for a new building in the college grounds. The brief called for residential accommodation and a lecture theatre/ performance space doubling as conference facilities during the vacations. The college asked for a building which would look good for many years and also feel 'mature' on first occupation.

The immediate context contained two buildings by Howell, Killick, Partridge and Amis as part of their 1960's masterplan, Hartland House by Giles Gilbert Scott (1938) and the Dining Hall by Gerald Banks (1953).

The completion of the HKPA masterplan was no longer felt by the client to be appropriate and we explored a number of options for the site of the building with the College Development Committee. The preferred option was to place the new building across the college grounds to complete the fourth side of a formal lawned quad with those earlier buildings. To the south of the new building, the retained Victorian villas and

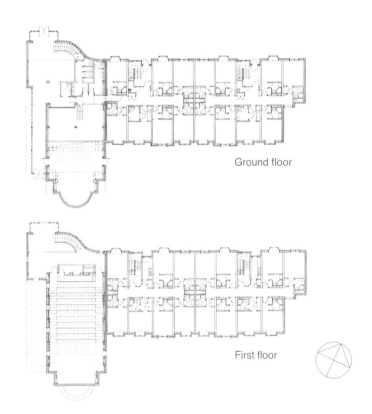

Ground floor

First floor

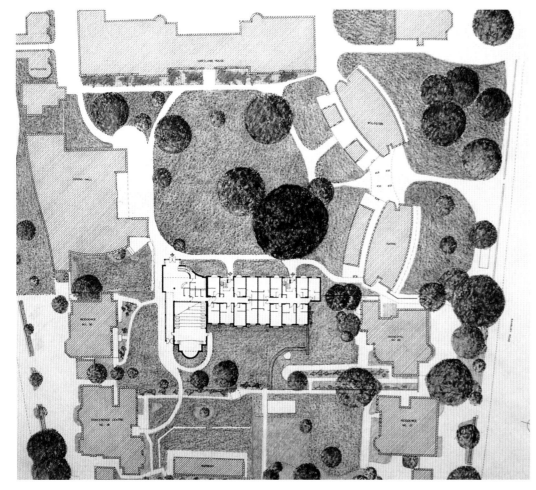

their gardens along Woodstock and Banbury Roads could create a series of less formal landscaped enclosures.

The accommodation includes 45 en-suite study bedrooms arranged around staircases in traditional Oxford college pattern.

In addition, a 150 seat auditorium with fixed and raked seating, suitable for both lecture use and performing arts, is provided. The apsidal end is a piano store. To ensure excellent acoustics for both the spoken word and music recitals, the volume of this room and the wall panel design were carefully considered. Fresh and tempered air is provided by a displacement air system with low velocity fans, in a basement plantroom, creating minimum noise.

The external elevations are of handmade bricks with natural stone elements such as bays and cornices. Pitched roofs are of Westmoreland slate and all external joinery is European oak. Materials are designed to give the building an early maturity.

North elevation

The new building was named after Claire Palley, Principal at the time of commissioning.

Dr Alan Alport who chaired the College Development Committee said:

The resulting Claire Palley Building, provided an immensely successful solution to our requirements, and the College derives the greatest satisfaction and pride from our continuing day-to-day use of the building. The overall design of the accommodation, lecture theatre and associated foyer/picture gallery is extremely handsome and effective, and the detailing is superb.

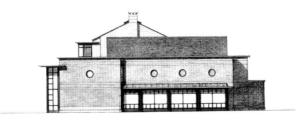
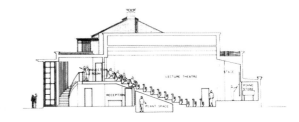

In their document *Shared Interest* (2007)
English Heritage commented:

> *The new residential and teaching
> block is exemplary. The architects
> have achieved an intelligent response
> to the subtle challenges of the
> complex historical environment.*

ss *Great Britain* and its historic dockyard Bristol 2006

The ss *Great Britain*, the world's first iron-hulled, screw propeller-driven, steam-powered passenger liner is the forerunner of virtually all modern shipping. Designed by Isambard Kingdom Brunel, she was, at her launch in 1843, at the cutting edge of available technology.

During her life at sea, the ss *Great Britain* crossed to America as a passenger liner, made many journeys to Australia and carried troops and horses to the Crimean war. At the turn of the century she was abandoned in the Falkland Islands, but in 1970 was brought back to the Listed dry-dock where she had been built.

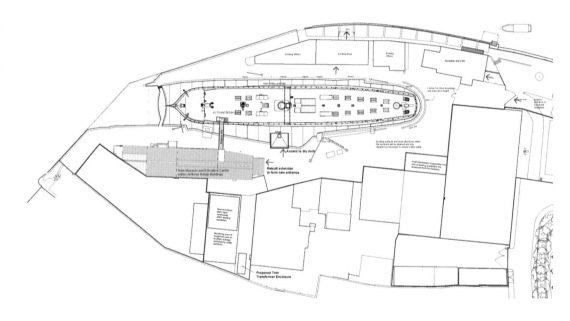

ss *Great Britain* returns home in 1970. Picture courtesy of *Bristol Evening Post*

Over subsequent years the corrosion of the salt-saturated iron hull accelerated and the long term survival of the ship required a new approach. This was to be accompanied by an authentic restoration of much of the ship's fabric, including extensive fitting out of the interior. The client's ownership of the Great Western Dockyard also provided an opportunity to reinforce awareness of the ship in context, and the conservation of dockside buildings was to include a new museum and other elements.

Research work had discovered that a reduction of relative humidity to 40 per cent slows the corrosion dramatically and a reduction to 20 per cent halts it entirely. To achieve this, a glass plate was installed at 'water level', forming a seal between the ship's hull and the dry dock wall and allowing the air below to be dehumidified. This waterline plate was then covered with a 50mm layer of flowing water extracted from the adjacent harbour. This acts to cool the glass plate as well as giving a sense that the ship is once again afloat.

A new timber and steel entry pavilion enhances the experience of going below the waterline and also controls humidity. Using the stairs, or a platform lift, visitors can fully explore the dock, the ship's hull, the original caisson holding the harbour water out and the dehumidification plant.

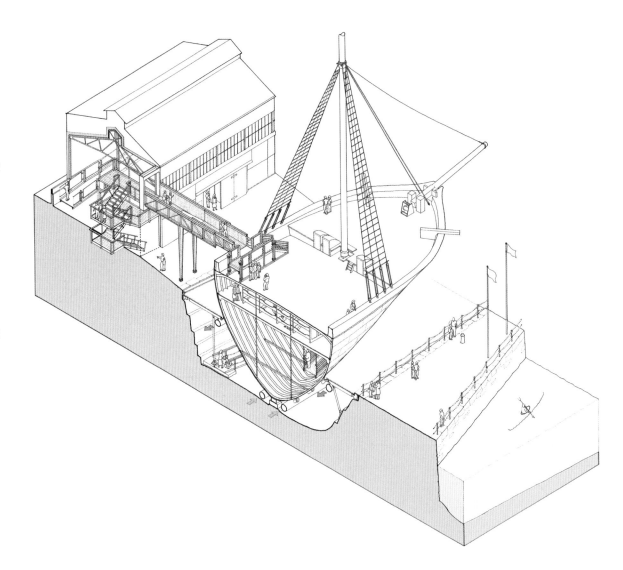

The glass plate is supported on trapezoidal section steel beams, fixed back to the dock walls on resin anchors. Glass tapered beams span between the steels to support the edges of the glass plates, whilst minimising the visual impact of the structure. A special seal was developed in Hyperlon, to seal the plate to both hull and dock wall. Essential repair work to the dry dock and caisson were carried out in close collaboration with English Heritiage. The supporting of the glass plate and the necessary ducts, nozzles and dehumidification machinery are enjoyed as innovative engineering complementary to that of the ship itself.

The project also included the conversion of the existing range of dockside buildings, built in 1914 and 1920, into a new museum, an education room, a small exhibition gallery and new access onto the ship. The workshop character of these is retained and with minimum intervention to its much adapted exterior, which reflects the changes in its ship repairing history. The end result was to 'look as if reasonably well maintained over the years'. Within, a new ramp takes the visitor through a series of time gates, finally arriving at the new bridge onto the deck, as passengers and crew would originally have boarded, a contemporary reinterpretation of such structures. The museum houses several large original artefacts such as the 32 metre main yard and the 17 tonne stern rudder frame

complete with a full-size replica propeller. Extensive interpretation allows visitors to understand the different phases of the ship's history and how it felt to be on board

Within the ship itself, there has been extensive restoration of both public rooms and individual cabins, whilst essential strengthening works, the ductwork for further dehumidification, and full disabled access provision have been discreetly integrated with minimum alteration of the original structure.

The significance of the brief and working with clients

Buildings are major investments for clients, as much in terms of what they are expected to deliver as in what they cost and good client architect relationships based on trust and understanding are a crucial component of all good buildings. Developing and interpreting the brief, with a broad definition of that, has always been a key part of our approach. Clearly our role is to advise, to challenge preconceptions where necessary, to bring our creativity and experience and offer alternative options, but all based on listening carefully and probing so as to understand what is really crucial to the success of their business or activity and indeed what might meet their dreams. David Sproxton, founder of Aardman Animations, has described our work as trying to understand their DNA.

Sometimes clients do not initially understand the complex and holistic nature of our role, expecting us to concentrate on the 'Architecture', by which they mean only the external appearance. We talk to our clients about the intrinsic nature of spaces, about the most appropriate ambience, about how good buildings, whilst not determining human behaviour, can suggest and facilitate appropriate actions.

We have been fortunate to work with many committed and inspiring clients with clear aspirations for their projects. The director of the Bristol Royal Society for the Blind had a vision of how the partially sighted could be helped to have a much more independent way of life. The new centre would promote self confidence and encourage these aspirations. The owners of Sheepdrove organic farm wanted a building that would be the heart of their farm, inspirational, highly sustainable and reinforcing their passion for the organic movement. The chair of Bristol's Millennium Project wanted public spaces 'suitable for both celebration and contemplation' and materials that would last 100 years. The director of the ss *Great Britain* Trust had a clear vision of the restored ship protected from long term decay and displayed in its historic dockyard in ways which would both delight visitors and inspire a new generation of innovative engineers. The Trustees of the Penny Brohn Centre were looking for an atmosphere of peace and tranquillity to help and support those with cancer. The directors of Aardman explored with us the essential nature of their business and how the exchange of ideas both formally and informally was key to their future.

All saw new buildings and structures as key to the realisation of their visions and were able to develop, with us, briefs which met both their physical requirements and their less tangible aspirations. By their responses to the built results we are re-assured that the buildings have met those aspirations.

It's rather better than a dream come true
Peter Lord, director
Aardman Animations

Whilst some clients, often representing bigger organisations, may not be as open to such discussions, our experience is that the conversations are always worth having. Good design can be understood and valued if properly explained – something we as a profession have not always been good at.

Developers do not always have a good press, but we have worked with a number who have been supportive of good contemporary architecture and prepared to fight the cause.

At Thornbury Peter Martin of Grosvenor Estate encouraged our knitting together of the existing fabric rather than the wholesale demolition proposed by the local authority. At Redcliff Quay, Peter Henwood of Standard Life strongly supported our proposals in the face of planning opposition. The late Euan Cresswell, client for a number of our Bristol projects, believed that he had a responsibility to contribute to the places he worked in and looked for good quality contemporary design.

The best clients are often the most demanding but building up that essential trust and mutual understanding is key to good buildings.

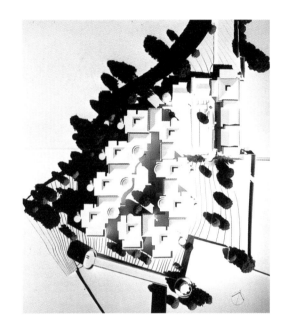

In an age when we take advantage of what computers can offer, we also remain enthusiasts for the hand sketch and the white card model as ways of exploring concepts within the design team and effectively engaging with the client.

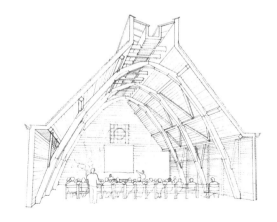

King Edward's Junior School Bath 1990

This Bath school for about 200 pupils was moving from an historic building in the city centre to an open sloping site on the edge of the city. The Head wanted a traditional arrangement of classrooms but emphasised the importance of the library as a focus.

A top-lit library became very much the heart of the new school with classrooms directly relating on half levels, taking advantage of the contours of the site. The library is immediately visible from the entrance and reception area and opens out in plan providing good places for study and clear supervision.

The arrangement of the classrooms in echelon form provides a threshold area to each classroom – as a gathering space at the beginning of the day and where coats and bags are stored. A display case encourages each class to display their current projects to the rest of the school.

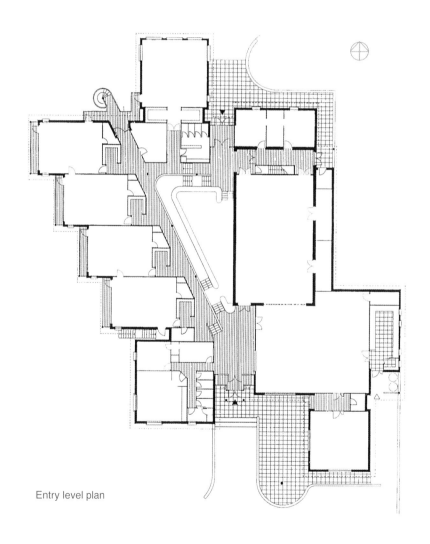

Entry level plan

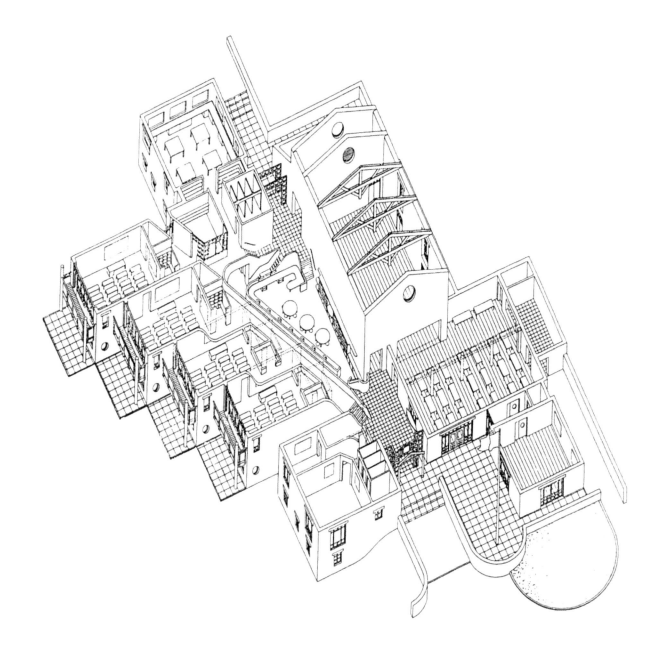

The building uses stone coloured block-work and pitched slate roofs with the different elements clearly articulated.

The entrance is designed to provide an appropriate sense of welcome and arrival for pupils and their parents.

Classroom doors and the main hall incorporate stained glass by Ros Grimshaw.

The RIBA Award Jury described the school as:

An excellent and inspiring example of architecture in the service of education. We particularly liked the quality of thought which the architect has brought to the organisation of the school and the way it appropriately and sympathetically occupies and exploits its site. We wish that all children could receive the opportunity to commence their education in a school as well designed and built as this one.

Faculty of Education University of the West of England Bristol 2001

The University of the West of England wanted to relocate its Faculty of Education from central Bristol to its main Frenchay campus.

Following a competitive selection procedure we were appointed to undertake feasibility studies for a new building as part of a new masterplan for the southern end of Frenchay Campus. The masterplan showed that in addition to the Faculty of Education there was also potential for new sports and arts facilities.

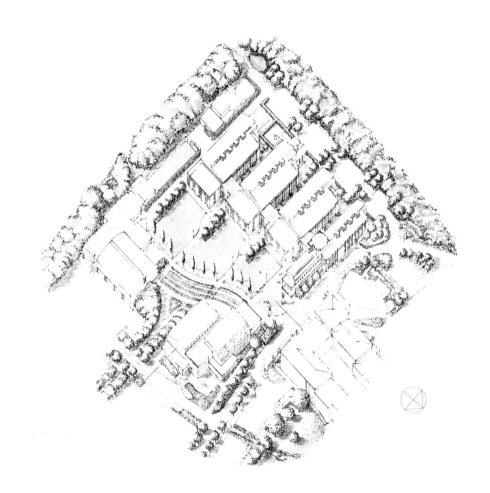

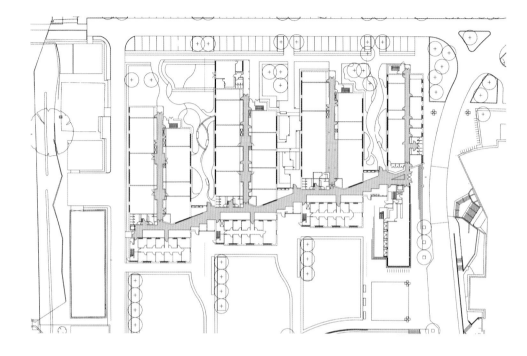

We recognised from the outset that the project's success would depend partly on the integration of the new building's circulation with the existing campus routes. To this end we proposed a wide and interesting 'street' through the Faculty rather than the conventional internal corridors provided generally across the academic departments. This street was to become a key element in the success of the new building in creating a social and academic space to exhibit work and meet people informally. The client justified this additional circulation space by these additional uses.

The street links a series of two-storey teaching wings to the west and 'houses' containing staff rooms to the east. A café is provided at the main point of entry from the rest of the campus to the north. Circulation at first floor is by a gallery to the street with linking bridges.

The teaching wings are designed for flexibility with demountable partition walls and extensive perimeter windows for maximum natural light. Teaching spaces are naturally ventilated except where Design and Technology workshops require mechanical extract plant.

The need to maximise the perimeter of the building led to an articulation of the overall plan into its separate volumes allowing us to develop a series of human scale pavilions and wings with transparent links. This scale is reinforced by the use of a palette of materials including timber cladding, facing blockwork and glass walls.

The street cuts through the building at an angle enabling one to see from one end to the other. The legibility of the building's organisation is enhanced by the top lighting that throws shadows across the space, ever-changing in the light.

Extensive landscaping includes raised lawns to the east with groups of trees framing distant views. On the west side of the street fingers of landscaping between the teaching wings each have a different character, from hard paving for sitting outside the café to soft courtyard planting.

Penny Brohn Cancer Care Bristol 2007

Bristol Cancer Help Centre was founded in 1980 and for over twenty years was based in Clifton. As a successful charity by 2000 it had outgrown its accommodation and the trustees were looking at sites in the Bristol area that would meet their needs, either in a new building or in an existing building with potential for development. Ham Green House, a Grade II Listed Building, formerly the Bright's family home and later owned by the NHS, is set in 4.5 acres of mature gardens dating back to the eighteenth century. Offering the potential for both reuse and extension it was purchased in early 2002. The move was encouraged by the Planning Authority and English Heritage as it would bring life back to an attractive listed building and gardens.

The brief for the enlarged facilities was drawn up in consultation with the trustees and staff who also sought advice from the Prince's Foundation, Prince Charles being a patron. The vision was always to create a centre with an atmosphere of peace and tranquillity which could help and support those with cancer. A visit to the centre whether for therapy, training or education, is expected to be an enlightening and

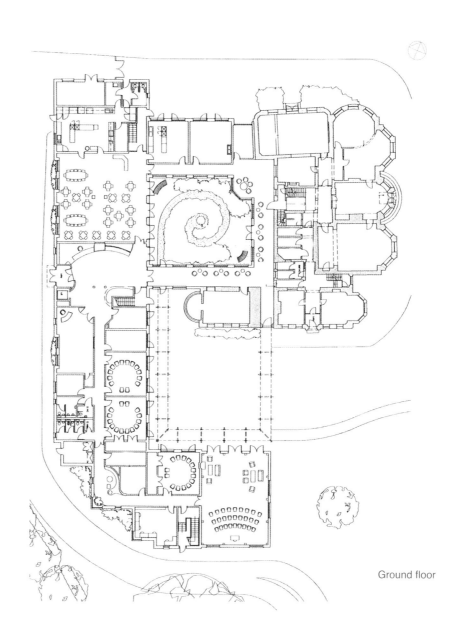

Ground floor

58

inspiring experience which stimulates fresh outlooks and ideas.

The extension to the original house acts as a protective form against the proximity of commercial buildings to the west and opens out to the tranquillity of mature landscaped gardens to the north and east.

The new building provides 26 en-suite bedrooms together with specially designed group rooms for the wide range of therapies carried out. The kitchens and dining room at the heart of the building reflect the importance of nutrition which extends to a purpose-built demonstration cookery room where courses can be run to teach the knowledge of appropriate nutrition from the charity's specialist team. There is also an in-house shop allowing residents and visitors to buy books, CD's,

skin care and recipe ingredients related to what they have learned during their visit. A large oak-framed structure creates a room for larger gatherings with the potential for general use as part of the integration of the centre into the local community. The existing refurbished house contains group rooms and a library with offices on the first floor.

The plan provides two courtyards, one cloistered and internal and the other semi-open to the gardens and distant views beyond. Between the courtyards sits a converted ancient stone barn which provides a peaceful sanctuary. The new landscaping includes oak pergolas with climbing and scented vines and honey-suckle, grassed lawns with seats for informal gathering and water features reflecting light and energy.

An eighteenth-century gazebo stands alone on the boundary looking out over the River Avon. This building, now fully restored, was used as a laboratory by Richard Bright whose work from here resulted in the discovery of Bright's disease.

The new building design is intended to have a 'comfortable' feel, avoiding the institutional and relating sympathetically to the existing house.

Centre for the Visually Impaired Bristol 1993

The Bristol Blind Asylum was founded in Callowhill Street Bristol in 1793 and was later to become the Bristol Royal Society for the Blind. Some 200 years later they began to plan a new centre for the visually impaired. A bold new vision was emerging and the director Bill Gold wrote:

Over the years attitudes towards people with visual impairment have changed. Rather than simply being labelled blind and therefore classified by their condition, people are encouraged to make the most of their residual vision and to aspire to an individual and normal way of living. The Centre would promote self-confidence and encourage these aspirations.

A site was purchased in Bedminster and after two years of research and design development work started on site in 1992.

This was a challenging brief for a unique building type. It demanded thorough research but published information was limited. Bill Gold arranged for us to visit different environments to gain insight and knowledge into the problems of visual

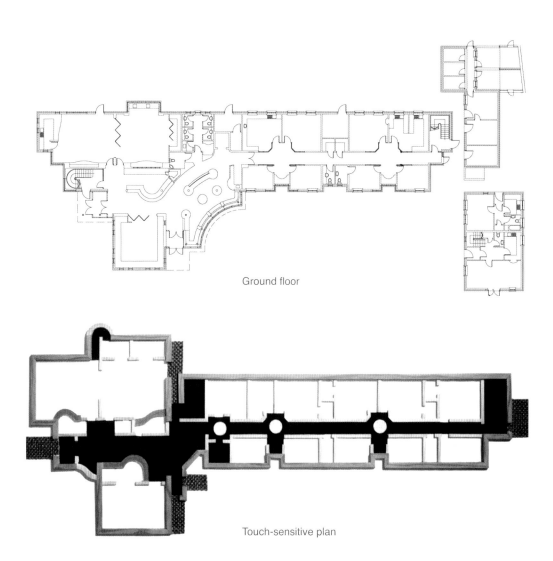

Ground floor

Touch-sensitive plan

impairment. On each occasion we were accompanied by sighted, partially sighted and blind members of the Society's staff. We observed and participated in the Society's daily activities including rehabilitation and training programmes with the visually impaired and education seminars with social workers and medical staff. We used the aids and equipment and, by wearing special goggles which simulated the visual effects of various eye conditions, it was possible to see how the environment is perceived by people with visual impairment. Our braille floor plans enabled us to guide fingertips over the arrangement of spaces and note comments and advice.

We learnt what to avoid, but also the positive contributions that design can make. Issues of a sense of arrival and of legibility are key, as are colour contrast, texture, light and shade, acoustics and materials.

The ground floor reception area includes activity rooms and a display shop enabling visitors to inspect and try out new technology and helpful gadgets. Built-in purpose-designed fixtures and fittings ensure there are no sharp edges or hazards created by the furniture. The acoustics have been carefully considered to avoid confusing reflections on entry where a welcoming atmosphere is very important. Beyond, there is a clear pattern of circulation with nodes, each giving access to four rooms. These nodes are designed to have side or top light with contrasting colours and floor textures and continuous wall rails guiding you to the door handles.

The landscaping complements the internal experience with careful choice of scented flowers and shrubs, the sound of water, good lighting and careful detailing.

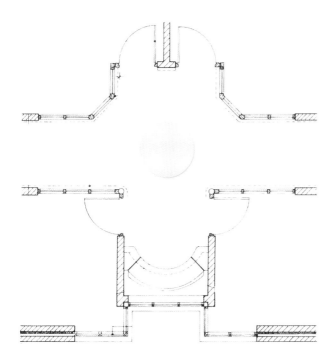

Circulation 'node' for building's legibility

City Learning Centres Bristol 2001

Bristol City Council received funds through
the Excellence in Cities initiative to provide
two specialist facilities for the learning of a
range of computer based technologies
before these could be made widely available in all schools.

The centres were to be based on two
Bristol secondary school sites but also
accessible to a group of primary and
secondary schools. After years of neglect of
the fabric of state education they were to
be seen as 'beacons' symbolising a new
period of investment.

With a passionate and knowledgeable
client team we developed the concept of a
variety of spaces that can be used in a
number of ways. Those at first floor are
clad largely in a translucent insulating panel
system whilst those at ground have limited
glazing both to limit distraction and
increase natural security.

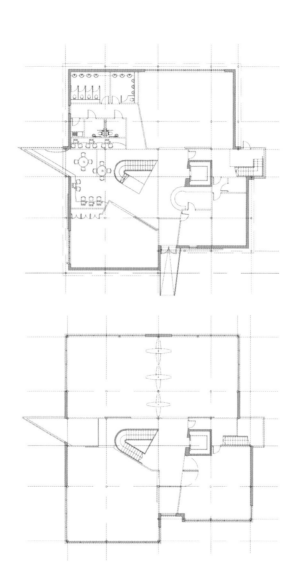

The central double height space unifies the building and provides focus and legibility. An angled 'prow' links both levels back to their immediate context and this also expresses the social function of this space. The translucent cladding provides high levels of natural light without compromising the use of computer screens and changes in appearance depending on the weather. Internally, sliding screens allow spaces to open up to the centre and an innovative pivoting storage system allows the two major spaces to be linked together.

The funding timetable required a very fast programme and from inception to completion was 39 weeks.

As beacons both centres are largely identical and only locally adjusted to their context.

In their citation for the awarding of the Prime Minister's Award for Better Public Buildings, the judges said:

The tremendous enthusiasm of the client, funding agency, and design and construction team have been rewarded with a practical, adaptable and delightful building that adds fun and motivation to school classroom learning...... This building represents the standards we should be aiming for across the country. Crisp, light, airy and staggering value for money.... A very, very interesting local but repeatable project that should give encouragement to all in the public service.

Theatre Royal Bristol

The Theatre Royal is the oldest continuously working theatre in the UK with a main auditorium dating from 1766 and linked to the former Coopers Hall of 1744.

Throughout the 1990s the Practice was appointed by the Board of Trustees of the Bristol Old Vic theatre company to act as architects for a number of forward-looking projects. These included funding applications from the Theatre Restoration Fund and work on Lottery applications for major refurbishment projects.

A number of feasibility studies included the extension of the site to Queen Charlotte Street for a new 800-seat theatre served by the existing entrance through the Coopers Hall in King Street.

Other studies showed that a major front-of-house rearrangement could enhance the theatre experience and give the option to restore the listed Coopers Hall to its original 1744 form. This would entail lowering the floor and replicating the staircase to enable the eighteenth century hall to be used again for a wide range of revenue-creating activities from drama to banqueting.

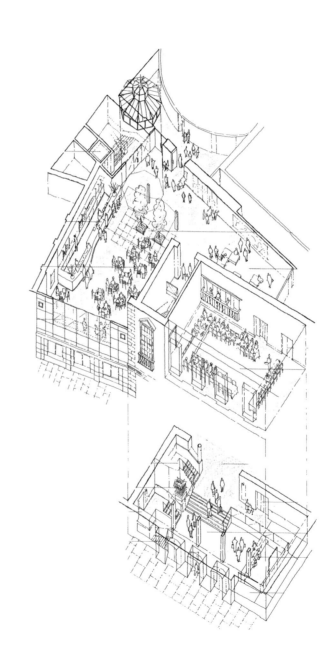

The lack of visual communication of the theatre with the street needed to be addressed and there was much discussion as to how this could be achieved. Our study showed how, by replacing the two storey infill between the Coopers Hall and 36 King Street with a three storey transparent kinetic wall, it would be possible to glimpse activity in the studio theatre from the street through suspended particle glass which switches to opaque when privacy is required.

A new building here would enable the principal first floor courtyard and bar to extend to the street and engage with the life and drama of King Street. The new second-floor accommodation would also engage the street with an education suite and corporate entertainment facilities. The existing offices would be relocated elsewhere.

These studies anticipated substantial remodelling but when all the buildings were listed Grade I in December 2000, the emphasis moved to restoring the existing buildings rather than major interventions.

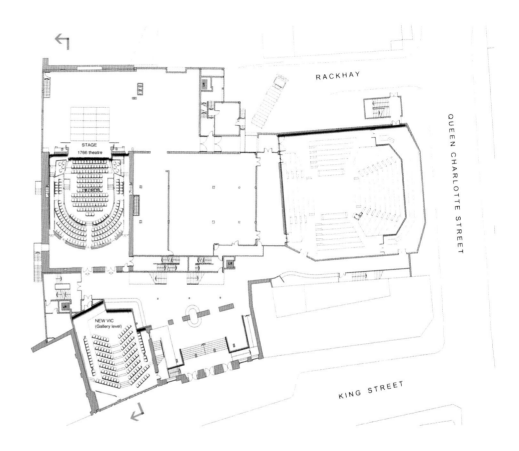

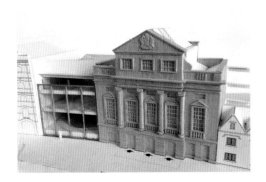

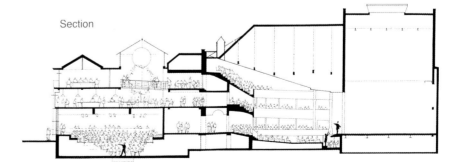

Section

Context

A considered approach to context is an important part of our thinking. We enjoy the opportunities to respond to the characteristics of a particular site and thus enrich the solution. There will be implications in the plan and the section and later in the choice of materials.

In addition to the context 'as found' we will have studied the history of the site and sometimes its archaeology, what Richard has called the layering of sites, all of which can provide inspiration and allow purposeful decisions. This self consciousness of the past, shared by many thoughtful contemporary designers, may in part reflect a realisation that we have had both the market forces and the means, particularly post war, to destroy much of the historic urban pattern. That earlier grain appears, in many cases, to have offered a better quality of urban environment, perhaps a more human scale and a good relationship between buildings and places. We have tried to restore some of those qualities of cities for people to enjoy.

A significant part of our work has been in Bristol – the adopted city for both of us and a city we feel a strong commitment to. Bristol has a rich, if fragmented, architectural history and a strong topography. Significant war damage, post-war clearance in the 60s, and poor commercial development have all contributed to some weakening of this legacy, but threats to fill in the docks, or allow very tall buildings

of poor quality, had produced an articulate and determined conservation movement by the time our 30 years began.

It is a movement we have respected whilst demonstrating, we hope, that new buildings of our own time can contribute to the sense of place without resorting to the all too prevalent pastiche or weak formulas. Good architecture of its time has often been opposed by contemporary popular taste and as architects we have to have the confidence to build what we believe in whilst always conscious of appropriateness.

We also have a responsibility to help our public to better understand new thinking, new issues and new materials. The Architecture Centre in Bristol, which we were instrumental in establishing in 1996, is very much about raising this public awareness, and thereby expectations, of good quality buildings and places of our age.

The concerns about architecture as object, prevalent in the 1960s and 1970s are equally critical today. We are concerned by the tendency of some clients to expect 'wow' factors and indeed inappropriately 'iconic' buildings, a slippery slope towards buildings as objects devoid of real meaning. Occasionally there will be quite legitimate 'objects', our relocatable Marketing Centre, symbolic of regeneration, or our City Learning Centres required to be 'beacons', but for us these are the exceptions.

Great George Street

One Bridewell Street

Redcliffe Quay

Responses to context must, of course, also include a proper consideration of the expression of use or cultural significance. Architecture is a holistic discipline.

The examples given here demonstrate the necessary range of a considered approach to context. They vary from the formal arrangement of Queen Square where a replacement restored a missing piece, to those where the new building restores, or sometimes provides, a new urban presence.

In the case of Great George Street we enjoyed the opportunity to demolish a 1960s slab block and to restore some of the grain you find in this fine Georgian street. On a highly prominent site in a sensitive Conservation Area the correct response was one of appropriate scale, form and use of the contours. Red brick, Bath stone and applied metal-work were the natural materials.

A few years earlier the design of One Bridewell Street required a very different response – one still related in form and scale to its context and also re-establishing street edges, but one where the use of a sophisti-cated metal rain screen cladding and a glazed atrium make a positive contribution to this otherwise rather bleak environment.

Our Redcliffe Quay office building fronting the floating harbour consciously picks up elements of the former brick warehouses destroyed in the war in terms of

scale and form and use of materials. Metal and timber balconies have a contemporary function but also reflect the former loading platforms, all a re-interpre-tation of the vernacular.

The student accommodation at St. George's Road reinforces earlier street edges and responds to local scale. This is also an example of how elevations should often be designed to be seen along the street. Here the proportion and depth of openings help to control and modulate the facade.

The Sheepdrove Conference Centre set in an Area of Outstanding Natural Beauty provides a different context where references are to the precedent of a 'long barn'. Its form nevertheless gives a clear expression of what this building is about, whilst the use of naturally weathering timber cladding helps the building to mature into its landscape.

We are conscious of Aalto's challenging statement that 'what matters is not what a building looks like when it is first built, but what it is like thirty years later.' The form, the weathering characteristics of materials and how they are detailed are all important and this remains an important preoccupation.

Responding to context has been an important source of inspiration.

St George's Rd

Sheepdrove

Offices, 31 Great George Street Bristol 1990

In 1988 we were offered the welcome opportunity to remove a 1960's eyesore on a prominent hillside position in the Brandon Hill Conservation Area. The existing seven-storey slab block could be seen sitting incongruously on this south facing hillside from most of the city centre and South Bristol.

The then owner required us to provide as much office space as the existing building and also asked us to consider an option for its refurbishment as a fall back, as, significantly, planning permission for earlier replacements had been refused. The site had not been built on historically, but terminates a row of substantial Georgian merchants houses rising up to Brandon Hill Park. There are extensive views over the city to the south and east and into the park to the south and west.

The appropriate response seemed to us to respect the building line and scale of the adjacent houses on the street, with lower floors set into the hillside and extending down the slope. Two, four-storey linked pavilions front the street with the lower floors organised around a courtyard on a series of stepped levels. All floors enjoy the views and the lower roofs provide planted terraces.

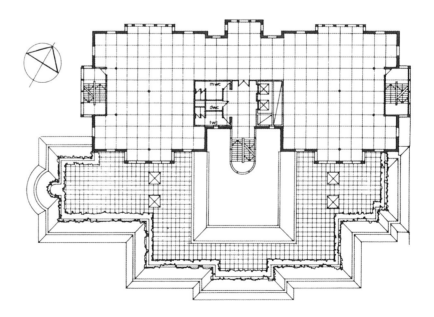

The building to be replaced

Given the immediate context and sensitivity, a soft red brick and Bath stone were the appropriate materials and have helped the building to mature into its context. The street elevation consciously relates to the scale, rhythm and key proportions of the Georgian terrace. A curved stone bay on the western elevation articulates a major internal meeting space and responds to views into and from the Park. The metal *brise soleil* applied here and to the southern elevations significantly reduces solar gain, and may also be seen to be reminiscent of the metal work applied to stonework elsewhere in Bristol.

Whilst initially designed speculatively, the building was further developed internally with Price Waterhouse Coopers who became the long term occupiers.

Before and, below, after

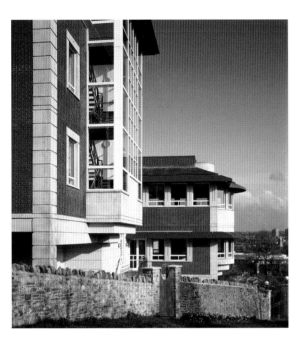

Arts Centre, the Last Invasion Centre Fishguard 1998

The trustees of the Last Invasion Tapestry, a significant work of art and craft created to celebrate the last invasion of the UK mainland – by Napoleon's troops in 1797 – were seeking new purpose built accommodation to display it in. We were selected by competitive interview for an Arts Council of Wales Lottery application.

The new building was to provide a permanent home for the 30-metre long tapestry in a controlled environment, an interpretation area and a gallery for contemporary arts and crafts. In addition there were to be artists' studios, educational facilities in a converted building, archive storage, retail space and a café opening on to a garden.

The site is in the centre of the Fishguard Conservation Area and was previously inaccessible to the public. The strategy incorporated a central top lit route linking both ends of this linear site, allowing access from an existing car park through to the town centre and engaging the public with all the activities of the centre.

The building was designed to be easily understood and to use controlled daylight in the gallery space. Locally-sourced materials and the work of artists and crafts people would have been integral to the design.

The project did not proceed when overall capital funding was reduced.

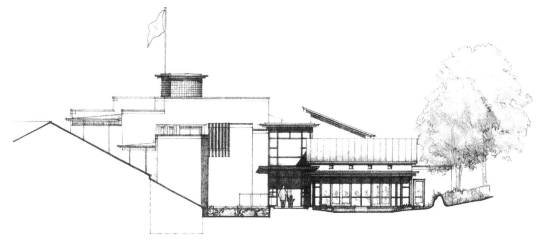

Front approach elevation

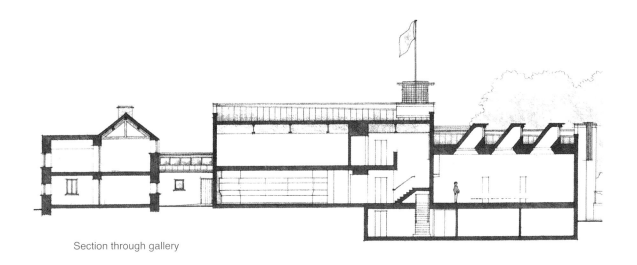

Section through gallery

Site context

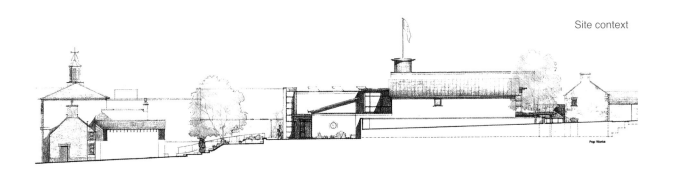

Student accommodation, Goldney Hall Bristol 1994

Thomas Goldney, a wealthy merchant and prominent
Quaker, built Goldney Hall on a south-sloping site in
Clifton in the eighteenth century. The house was substan-
tially altered in the nineteenth century by Alfred
Waterhouse but the ornate gardens, including ramparts,
look-out tower and shell grotto survive to this day and are
in the care of the University of Bristol.

In the mid 1960s, Architects Co-Partnership had designed
a student village on fields immediately below the historic
garden consisting of 180 rooms in self-catering flats each
arranged in groups of six rooms around a communal
dining area. Individual four- and five-storey towers were
grouped close together but detached from each other and
the space enclosed was not a recognisable 'place'.

With financial support and the close engagement of
Sainsbury's Linbury Trust, the University held a design
competition for the addition of a significant number of
new student rooms and the replacement or upgrading of
the existing which were no longer considered to meet
requirements.

We won the competition by proposing to retain and extend
the existing buildings, enclosing a new level courtyard
across the sloping site. For the main group of buildings their
retention and refurbishment, integrated with new additions,
seemed the most appropriate and sustainable solution.

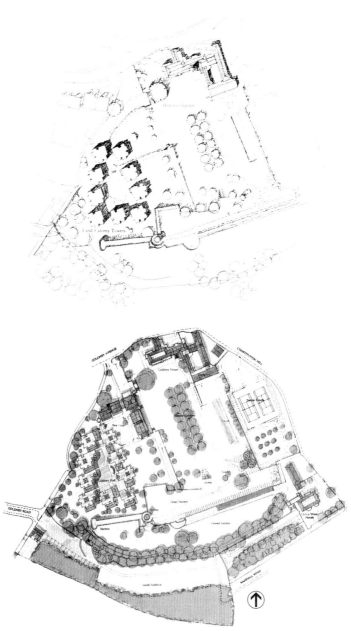

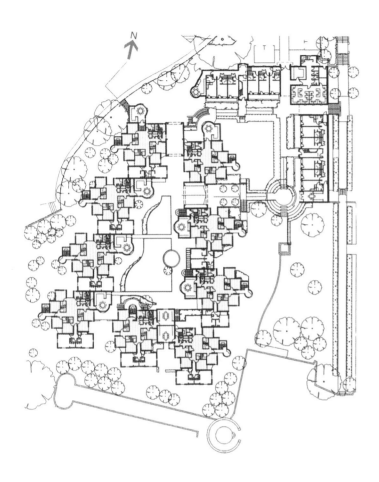

Existing buildings

Competition sketch of proposed courtyard from same viewpoint

Our analysis of the existing accommodation (innovative and award winning in its day) and how it worked socially, led us to propose an eight-room group supported by a generous new kitchen and dining area. These are readily accessed and visible social areas and are also clearly expressed in the external form of the building, encouraging easy interaction with the whole community.

The additions transform the overall form and also help unify the elevations as a whole. New fire escape staircases to the rear enjoy excellent views and have seats providing quiet places for reading and meeting.

A separate L-shaped two-storey building encloses an entry court and provides a much needed porters lodge, a computer and social room and 24 postgraduate rooms.

The new rear wall of random pennant stone forms an edge to the historic gardens on its historic boundary line. This is reinforced by an avenue of pleached limes.

Residential, Capricorn Quay Bristol 2002

Beaufort Homes had acquired this former timber yard site on the edge of the Floating Harbour as part of the overall regeneration of the city docks. Their brief called for mainly two bedroom apartments taking advantage of the extraordinary position on the bend of the floating harbour looking south across the water to Brunel's ship the ss *Great Britain* and beyond.

During the medieval period the site was on Canon's Marsh a part of the estate of St Augustine's Abbey (later Bristol Cathedral). At that time it would have stood on the River Avon approximately one kilometre to the west of the medieval docks. The site appears to have been developed for industrial purposes during the seventeenth

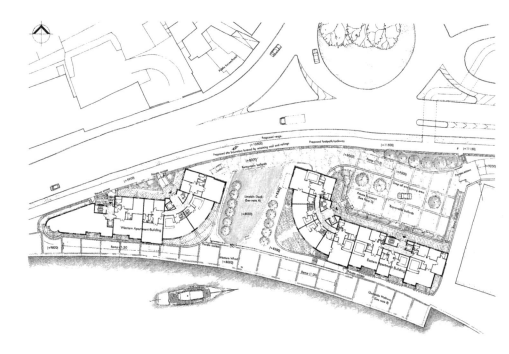

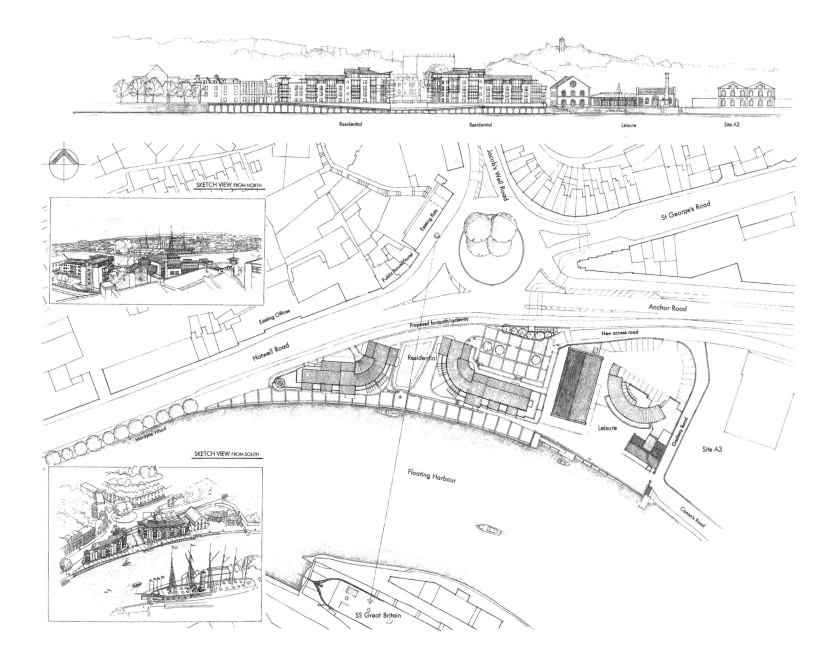

Residential

Residential

Leisure

Site A3

SKETCH VIEW FROM NORTH

Jacob's Well Road

St George's Road

Existing Boats

Public house/hotel

Anchor Road

Existing Offices

Proposed footpath/cycleway

New access road

Hotwell Road

Residential

Leisure

Mardyke Wharf

Site A3

Canon's Road

SKETCH VIEW FROM SOUTH

Floating Harbour

SS Great Britain

century when a mud dock, known then as the Limekiln Dock was formed. In the early twentieth century the Merchant Venturers sold the dock to the Great Western Railway Company to extend the Harbour railway into Canon's Marsh. In constructing the railway the dock was filled and a new wharf was constructed, using the then innovative Hennebique reinforced concrete.

The layout preserves the footprint of the old Limekiln Dock. This also maximises views up and down the harbour, provides a garden for residents and maintains views through the site from Hotwell Road to the ss *Great Britain*. The two curved buildings contain a total of 41 apartments and are planned to enable everyone to enjoy water views and lengthy periods of sun to living rooms and balconies. Careful acoustic detailing allows rooms looking north over the busy Hotwell Road to be adequately soundproofed.

The massing of the development was the subject of extensive discussions with planning officers. It was agreed that it was appropriate to create a form that sat comfortably along the waterfront respecting the folded topography of Cliftonwood behind and preserving views of Brandon Hill and Cabot Tower to the north from the deck of Brunel's ship.

The quayside walkway is lowered via ramps to make access to the old dock level and the boarding of the harbour ferry and larger boats possible.

The redevelopment of this classic brown-field site has cleared former polluted land, provided additional housing in the city centre and completed a missing link in the walkway along the Floating Harbour.

Student accommodation, St George's Road Bristol 2001

In seeking additional residential accommodation in the city centre the University of Bristol came to an agreement with the then Acton Housing Association to develop proposals for the former Royal National Institute for the Blind Workshop's site on St George's Road.

This former quarry posed interesting challenges for a dense development of about 360 ensuite rooms required by the brief. A courtyard form was developed.

We were reinstating earlier street edges on two sides and relating in scale to the two significant buildings east and west, the classical, Brunel-inspired, former hotel and at the upper end the Masonic Hall.

The site perimeter slopes from east to west and more steeply from south to north.

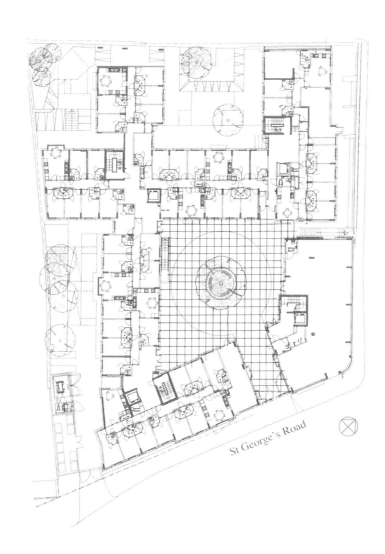

St George's Road

Student rooms, normally paired to efficiently use the plumbing and ventilation stacks, can produce an unfortunate external rhythm and scale. To avoid this and to recognise the way the elevations would normally be perceived, along the street, we developed a window within a larger recess where it is the scale and rhythm of the recesses that provides the appropriate urban scale. Where possible the communal kitchens are located on the street elevations and these are expressed as angled bays, not only increasing views out but expressing this key element of the accommodation.

By day and night the sight of students socialising contributes to the life of the street.

Residential and Offices, 22-25 Queen Square Bristol 2007

Our clients, Westmark, owned properties in the south east corner of this great square providing the opportunity to rebuild a missing corner and to add new residential behind.

Queen Square is the largest square in England after Lincoln's Inn Field and a key public space in the city. It was first laid out by the City Corporation in 1699, a bold piece of major urban planning. A geometric web of paths focus on an equestrian bronze statue of William III by JM Rysbrack.

The square has survived damaging riots and fires in 1831, the building of a diagonal dual carriageway in the 1930s and World War II bombing. Today, with the road removed, it has been re-landscaped and restored to its former glory and tranquillity.

To allow the diagonal road, the south east corner house, number 25, had been removed whilst numbers 22 to 24 had been largely rebuilt following war damage. The ashlar facade and staircase of number 22 was the only remaining historic fabric.

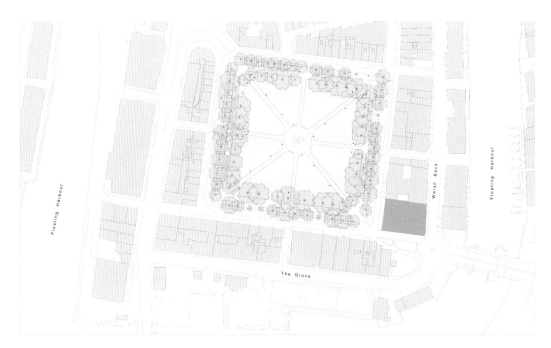

Number 25 before the road

Here was a clear, and rare, example of how faithful reconstruction on the Square was the only appropriate option.

The historic pattern had warehouses opening onto quaysides behind the merchants houses. In this case new residential could be built on former ware - house land without the restraints of the Square itself but respectful of the context.

The rebuilding of number 25 was based on old photographs, maps and drawings of other Queen Square houses. We worked closely with conservation architects Donald Insall and Partners and under the watchful eye of English Heritage.

The rest of the site provides 34 apartments all enjoying good views over the Floating Harbour and of St. Mary Redcliffe.

A framed structure with timber cladding infill acts as a transition to the rebuilt number 25. The brick clad building which turns the corner acknowledges, in its overall form, the nearby substantial, brick warehouses with their projecting bays. The main residential entrance is marked by a patinated copper bay surmounted by a loggia.

Library Extension, University of Bath 1996

In 1994 the University of Bath wished to extend the main library onto the central Parade and convert the whole facility to a 24-hour study centre. The brief aimed to provide an additional 550 reading spaces and computer terminals and improve the overall quality of the working environment and its energy performance. The library, a 1960's CLASP System building, occupies a prominent site at the heart of the university campus and the brief recognised the potential of its strategic location to be transparent and to 'shine like a beacon', welcoming visitors throughout the day and night.

Our 'glass box' solution, won in a limited design competition, resolved a major engineering challenge. Structural constraints were imposed by the existing building and the lightweight elevated deck of the Parade only offered six load bearing columns at basement level which would have to be reinforced to take the new floors above. Furthermore no access for construction plant could be allowed on the Parade except from each end of the 41 metre frontage. The extension would have to be built from each end, with cranes located in existing light wells, only giving access to the lower road level for all deliveries of plant and materials.

The structural solution of a lightweight transparent envelope supported by an independent steel balanced cantilever structure allowed an extra six metre bay to be built over the Parade supported on the six existing concrete columns. By reinforcing these existing columns it was possible to support six new cruciform steel masts

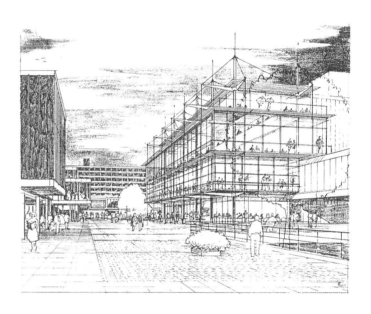

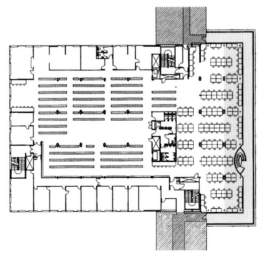

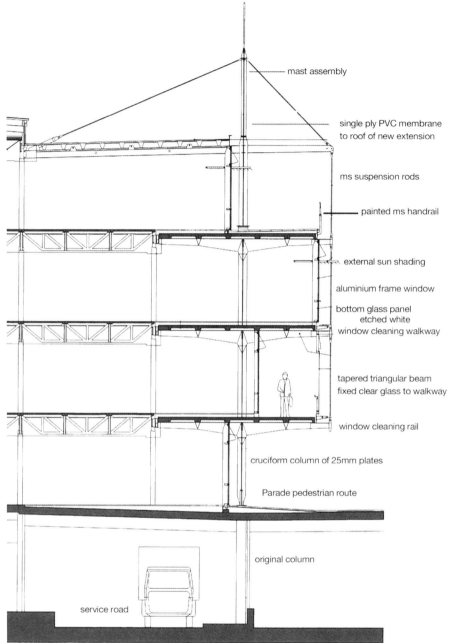

mast assembly

single ply PVC membrane
to roof of new extension

ms suspension rods

painted ms handrail

external sun shading

aluminium frame window

bottom glass panel
etched white

window cleaning walkway

tapered triangular beam

fixed clear glass to walkway

window cleaning rail

cruciform column of 25mm plates

Parade pedestrian route

original column

service road

Section showing steel balanced cantilever designs

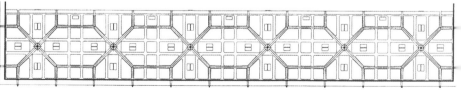

Reflected ceiling plan

with diagonal arms and horizontal edge beams supporting coffered precast floor units. The resulting visual effect of the masts from below is reminiscent of a row of trees.

The south façade of the extension is visually articulated with storey-height glazing, steel masts and *brise-soleil*. Shading the south facing elevation is done by a variety of devices. At Parade level the extension is protected by an overhanging walkway which connects a corridor system around the campus. Areas of etched glass, external *brise-soleil* and internal light shelves combine to reduce direct solar gain and glare whilst retaining a high level of natural light and the spectacular views of the surrounding countryside.

The new building is an extension of a much larger envelope and the new displacement air system maintains a comfortable working environment for the whole building.

Sustainability

From the perspective of 2010 where sustainability is key to all our work it is interesting to reflect on how these concerns have developed over the thirty years.

In the 1960s and 1970s there was little widespread awareness of the potential impact of climate change and with historically low fuel prices it was difficult to persuade clients of the need to spend money on more energy efficient buildings. Concern about the need to take a more responsible view about the sourcing and use of materials was only slowly emerging. It was an age of long term national plans based on assumptions about unlimited energy and market led growth.

The oil crises of the 1970s required a re-evaluation of these assumptions and Richard and I, in the years immediately before we joined forces, had opportunities to explore options for reducing significantly the energy consumption of buildings. Richard developed an innovative, relatively shallow plan form, for the offices at Broad Quay allowing natural ventilation to replace mechanical systems in the future. David, working with Sandy Wilson and Arups on a new HQ for Lucas Industries, developed forms which maximise roof lighting without summer solar gain whilst benefiting from low angle winter sun. With high insulation levels, exposed thermal mass and lower lighting levels than the norm this would have been an energy-efficient building.

Lucas HQ, section through top-lit domes

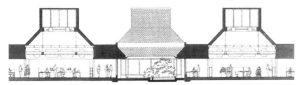

We were both aware of passive design approaches and Richard had developed house types exploring these concepts.

For some years though the imperative for finding sustainable solutions was not seen as a priority by society as a whole. The design of most office buildings for example was still governed by the need to meet 'institutional' standards – those laid down by remote pension companies who ultimately provide the finance for most developments. These were largely based on North American experience of air conditioned offices with air introduced at ceiling level, excessive light levels requiring high levels of ventilation and an expectation of a lighting controlled environment. Occupiers expected to be able to operate in short sleeves at all times even though there was growing evidence of disadvantages of air conditioned working environments. In the housing field clients, who would not themselves be paying the heating bills, were often reluctant to consider more energy efficient heating methods. Facilities managers often insisted on what they saw as more reliable methods of heating and cooling than opening windows.

However, progressive thinking was possible and in One Bridewell Street, completed in 1987, a series of design decisions provided a very low energy use for an air conditioned building which interestingly still compares very well in overall energy consumption with some of the best low energy buildings of recent years. Given its location between the two busy roads air conditioning was inevitable, but careful choice of equipment, lower lighting levels with good control, the use of the atrium

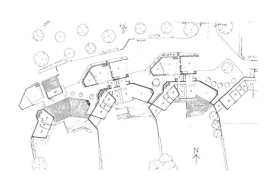

Passive solar housing, Ubley, with Peter Smith 1968

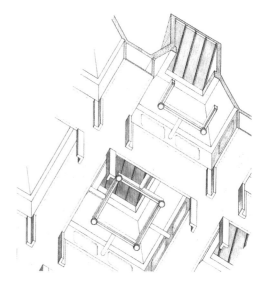

Lucas HQ, 1976

to preheat the office space, good insulation and thermal mass, coupled with excellent systems management in practice, contributed to a very energy-efficient building.

On the south elevation of Great George Street the *brise soleil* cut out high summer sun while maximising daylight. Here the air conditioning system was carefully zoned to allow individual offices to open their windows for natural ventilation and to enjoy their quiet site.

By 1992, working with Hoare Lea, we were using a displacement air system for a major office building for CMIG. As the air is introduced at low level it only requires to be a little cooler or warmer than the ambient temperature – significantly reducing energy use. It was also used in the performance space at St Anne's College, Oxford as it is also a very quiet method of ventilation.

Meanwhile the pressure to face up to the impact of climate change and the realisation that the peak oil we had talked about in the 1970s was finally becoming a future reality was leading to very different attitudes. Legislation, belatedly, required less wasteful solutions and the market recognised that building occupiers faced a future of increasingly expensive fuel. Even the conservative institutions behind bodies such as the British Council for Offices were persuaded to revise their expectations of office temperatures, lighting levels, etc.

Such changes allowed us to practice more widely approaches we had long advocated. Buildings were increasingly required to be sustainable on a broader front. We have all become much more knowledgeable about the responsible selection of materials, their embodied energy, sustainable forms of construction, control of waste and options for the re-use of materials. We developed a low energy proposal for the conference

centre at Sheepdrove Organic Farm. The client here had pioneered organic farming on a fairly large scale and wanted as sustainable building as possible in all aspects. The building is entirely naturally ventilated, including a conference space for 200 people, associated smaller spaces and a restaurant, using the height of the spaces and the effectiveness of roof lighting.

Designing new secondary schools to a brief requiring low energy solutions allowed us to develop with Arups our thinking on natural cross ventilation with each teaching space having a 'chimney'. Combined with the thermal mass of the exposed concrete soffits, these spaces have proved to keep acceptable conditions even in very hot weather.

Our Aardman Headquarters was the subject of much discussion on how best to maintain a good working environment which minimised energy use while accepting the likelihood of higher future temperatures. The mixed mode solution relies on natural ventilation for most of the year with maximum daylight reducing the need for artificial lighting. The planned rooftop wind turbines are not yet efficient enough to be worthwhile, but could be retro-fitted or replaced with photo-voltaics. The majority of the materials used are sustainable and use a high percentage of recycled content. Our Deanery Road headquarters for the Environment Agency has recently achieved the highest BREEAM rating in 2010 for an office building in the UK.

Developing low energy and sustainable buildings continues to be a major challenge for design teams and contractors, but the absolute necessity to address these issues in existing buildings as well as new is now well established and real progress is being made.

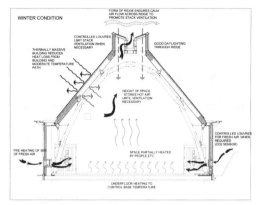

Sheepdrove Farm, conference centre

Offfices, One Bridewell Street Bristol 1987

In 1984 we were commissioned by MEPC to design the south west regional offices for tenants Arthur Young (now Ernst and Young) in an apparently inauspicious site surrounded by noisy city centre roads and 1960's development. The client's brief called for a high profile design with considerable flexibility in use and an excellent professional working environment.

The six-storey building is designed to make a clear statement of its purpose and to be clearly legible to those using it. Most of the accommodation is contained in an L-shaped plan around a full height, glazed entrance atrium of south east orientation. The main reception is located in this space which is overlooked by circulation galleries from which dramatic views of the city are gained. Passers-by have views into the atrium and at night the space provides a beacon of light within this somewhat gloomy area.

The atrium also provides beneficial preheating giving an environmental transition as well as an acoustic buffer to the surrounding traffic.

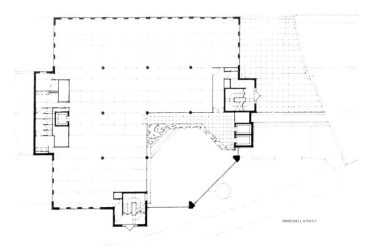

BRIDEWELL STREET

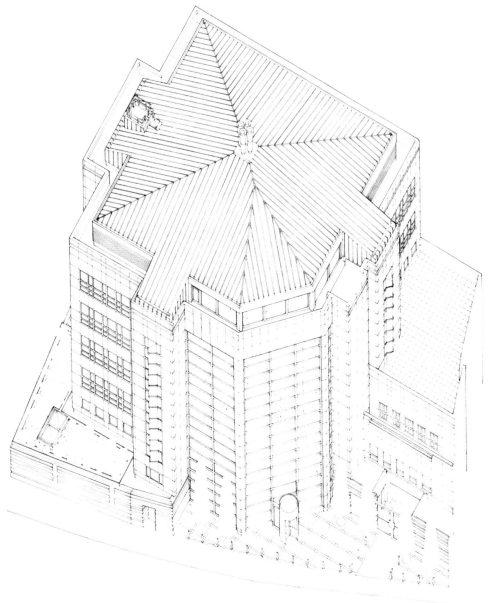

A three-storey wing links the new building with the Bay Horse public house creating a transitional scale to this late Victorian architecture.

This city location required the use of air-conditioning, principally for acoustic purposes and a conventional VAV installation with plant in the roof space was designed, using the atrium as a return air path. Using highly efficient equipment, lower lighting levels than the then current norms with sensor control, and with committed management, very low energy consumption was achieved. The building was the subject of a BRE Energy Efficiency in Offices Good Practice Case Study, of May 1991. The paper concluded:

> *By attention to every stage from inception through to management, One Bridewell Street demonstrates that high comfort standards and modest running costs can be obtained using proven and readily available technology, without any particularly remarkable energy saving architectural or engineering features.*

The low energy consumption achieved then still compares very favourably with current low energy buildings.

One Bridewell Street is appreciated as a bright, contemporary building in a rather dull context. The cream aluminium rain screen cladding and red framed curtain walling give a lightness which reflects by day and glows at night. The form of the roof and specially designed flues have added a positive element to the city's roofscape.

The atrium tree sculpture by Terry Powell is made from small standard aluminium tubular sections and egg-crate mesh and was assembled on site.

The Kindersley Centre Lambourn 2005

The owners of the 2,500 acre Sheepdrove Organic Farm in Berkshire, Peter and Juliet Kindersley, wanted a conference and education centre.

We won a limited ideas competition and our close creative dialogue with them was key from the outset. The building was to be highly sustainable and is located in an Area of Outstanding Natural Beauty.

Working with the mechanical engineers, it became clear that a naturally ventilated conference space for 200 people, together with associated breakout spaces and a restaurant, could be achieved given careful attention to the cross section and very simple cooling or heating of the incoming fresh air. The concept of a 'long barn' had some resonance in terms of both use and context and the largely exposed Douglas fir frames were developed by Mark Lovell, an innovative structural engineer with whom we have worked on a number of projects. These 'arches' of largely solid timber carry the load directly to the ground with a minimum of metal work. They are a major feature of the conference space but also form the primary structure throughout the main building.

First floors are inserted where necessary for additional meeting spaces and the upper part of the restaurant. The ventilating ridge also provides

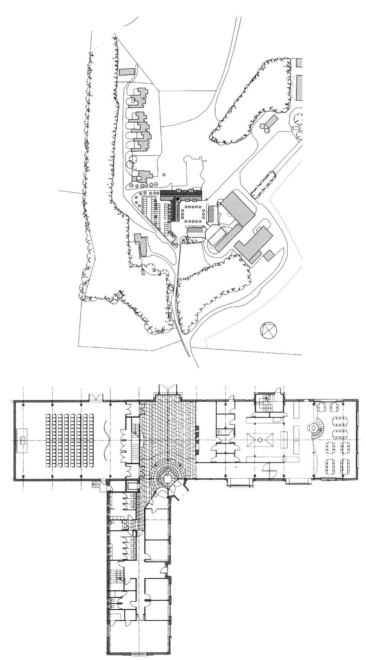

UPPER
DINING ROOM

extensive top light. Oak-framed, double-height bays and a three-storey drum provide focal points both externally and internally, whilst cedar shiplap cladding and cedar shingles help the building to weather into its landscape.

At right angles a wing of offices and further meeting rooms is conventionally framed and finished in lime render; it forms the fourth side of a new, paved yard.

The building is partly dug into the chalk and a rammed chalk wall forms one wall of the main conference space, providing good insulation and a degree of structural stability, and demonstrating the potential for such sustainable materials.

Aardman Animations Headquarters Bristol 2009

The Bristol-based, Oscar-winning, animation house required a new headquarters. It was then occupying a former banana warehouse and a number of temporary buildings on the adjacent land it owns. The directors wished to stay on Spike Island – an area they closely identify with.

After a limited competition we were invited to prepare an overall masterplan to include new accommodation for about 200 people and with options for selling parts of the site for future housing and redeveloping the banana warehouse site.

To more fully understand the nature of their organisation, we embarked upon an intensive and creative dialogue with both the directors and the heads of the various departments which continued throughout the final development of the headquarters building itself. The exchange of ideas was clearly key to their success and a new building needed to help facilitate that process, often unplanned and informal. Most of their activities, creative and administrative, take place in office type space (large-scale production takes place in industrial sheds on the edge of the city).

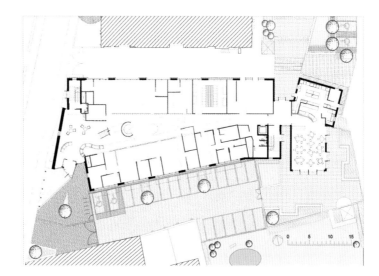

Ground floor

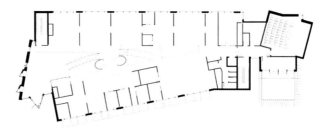

First floor

Looking at other recent buildings with the client led to the concept of a series of linked 'rooms' retaining flexibility in layout but also a sense of identity for working groups of six to nine people. This approach also produces significant areas of wall space for Aardman's extensive display of working images.

The main circulation is placed in the public realm outside a series of 7.5 metre x 7.5 metre bays. A clear brief to reduce energy, as part of a sustainable approach, justified a central three-storey atrium providing significant extract ventilation and controlled daylight. The site has two natural edges at approximately 11 degrees to each other and placing the two office wings either side of a tapered atrium offered a number of benefits. Breakout spaces and a gently curved laminated timber staircase occupy this space and there are many opportunities here for Aardman expression of their own very special character.

Externally the building uses strongly contoured larch and sweet chestnut which, when weathered, will retain the visible structure of the elevations. The building presents its most public face to Gas Ferry Road. Here, glazed block and copper clad bay windows intended

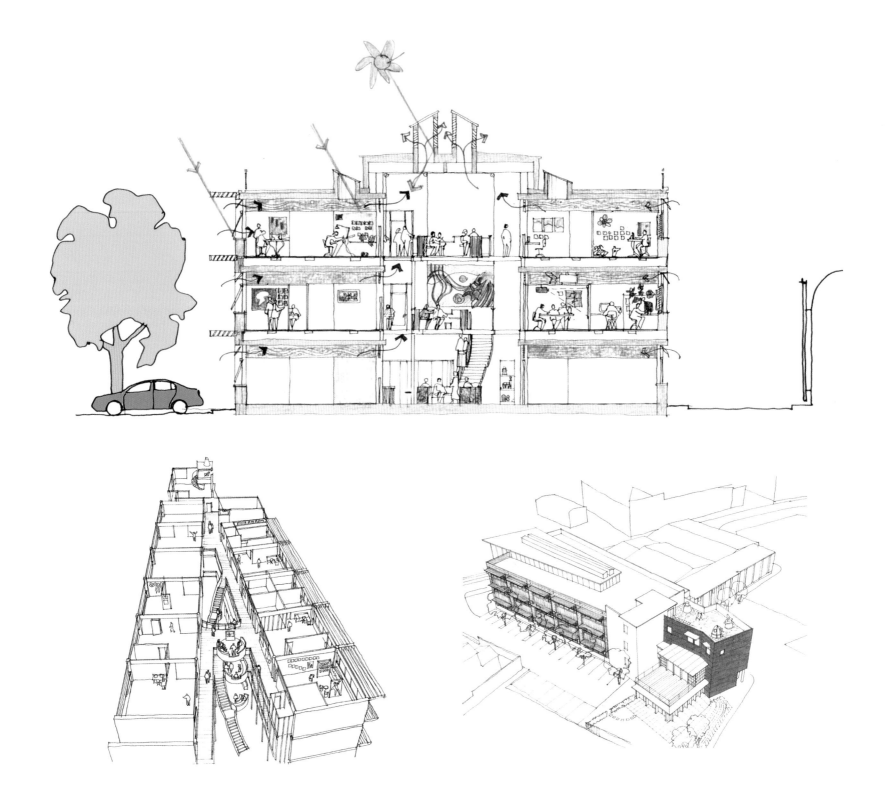

for display provide its urban presence. The other end containing special spaces such as a viewing theatre and the canteen is placed at an angle and clad in copper.

A garden outside the canteen, a grassed roof, accessible at first floor and a roof terrace provide additional social space on this tight urban site.

The RIBA Jury commented:

The form and scale of the building responds to the historic industrial nature and grain of the site whilst a creative and free approach to the window distribution on the public face allows unexpected and tantalising glimpses of the interioe and provides a showcase for some of the production company's iconic characters.

This is a crafted and wholly considered three-dimentional democratic space which promotes and celebrates fun on equal terms with efficiency, and community and belonging on equal terms with private space and work. Every office space in every city should be this good.

Henbury School Bristol 2005

Bristol was one of the first authorities to take advantage of the Labour Government's plans to invest in the rebuilding or significant refurbishment of the nation's secondary schools neglected for many years. These were largely to be done through the Private Finance Initiative, a process involving a competition between contractors and their design teams.

We worked with HBG Construction (later BAM) on two schools – Henbury and Monks Park and developed the detailed briefs with the schools and the authority. Budgets were significantly lower for these early PFI's, when compared to the following 'Building Schools for the Future' programme, so value for money was paramount. The Authority used our City Learning Centres as a benchmark for design quality within tight budgets. This was very early in the rebuilding programme with architects and educationalists only gradually appreciating how radical changes to some of the types of space in schools could assist quite new forms of learning. Whilst these designs are therefore fairly conventional from the perspective of 2010, they were part of that developing process and have achieved far better learning environments than the

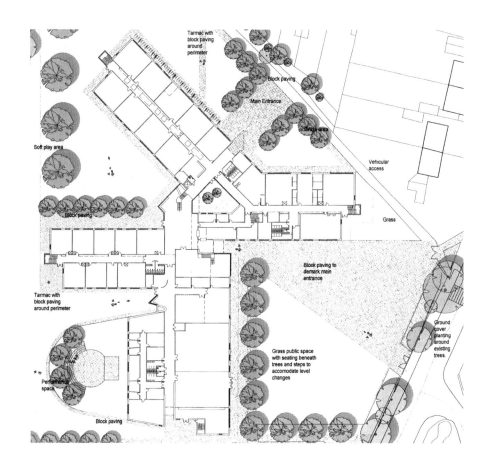

schools they replaced. They have been warmly welcomed by staff, students and parents.

Henbury has an immediately legible plan with a series of wings radiating from a double height reception, display area and social heart for the school. Landscaping provides soft and hard areas for recreation and socialising. The new school is more visible than the old from the main road and is set behind a landscaped area suitable for community events and displays.

A new community leisure centre with pool, gym and fitness suite is also provided on the site and shared with the school.

Masterplanning and Urban Design

Leslie Martin, our professor at Cambridge, once commented that he saw no necessary distinction in the approach of an architect between the design of a teaspoon and the development of a masterplan. Whilst this may be challenged in an age of increasing specialisation, we have found it both possible and rewarding to move from the design of individual buildings to the development of masterplans and the broader considerations of urban design.

As we have noted earlier, individual buildings should always contribute to their context, but masterplanning, or the design of larger pieces of cities, frees us from the constraints of the red line around individual planning applications and allows us to think about spaces, relationships and issues of grain and texture on a wider scale.

Good master planning is very much about the making of places that people can enjoy and make good use of. We need to be aware of relationships to the wider context in terms of patterns of use, future changes and potential linkages. There can be opportunities for providing places of varying nature, effective networks of pedestrian and cycle routes, integrated public art, new visual connections and improving links with and enhancing the green infrastructure. Shared spaces for people and vehicles are re-emerging as valuable components of a better environment for all of us. Urban design in terms of choosing appropriate forms, scale, materials and expression is the further development of masterplanning. At the microscale good materials, street furniture and light fittings all add to good enjoyable places.

Masterplanning and urban design involves close working with other disciplines – planners, landscape architects, artists, traffic specialists and many others – but architects can play a key role in seeing and coordinating the broad picture.

In Bath we developed proposals for the Southgate shopping area, adjacent to the railway station, which not only introduced new public spaces of some scale, but also tackled the challenge of reinterpreting Bath's architectural traditions. Given the strength of the preservation movement in that city it was not surprising that the scheme proved controversial, but there was also a strong lobby in support.

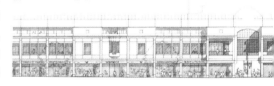

Southgate, street elevation

Southgate, view from Beechen Cliff

The recently completed redevelopment by others some twelve years later takes a different approach.

Part of the thinking behind the proposals for Canon's Marsh (developed as part of Concept Plannng Group, see page 135) were to make this a seamless extension of the adjoining areas of the City. An initial idea to reroute Anchor Road proved too disruptive to what, for now, remains a major arterial route, but we nevertheless provided important links. The principle of a strong pedestrian route from Temple Meads station to the ss *Great Britain*, symbolically provided a missing link in Brunel's planned journey between London and New York, linking two of his great Bristol achievements. Integrating new uses, existing buildings, new spaces and relationships to the harbour have helped this previously derelict area to become a natural part of the city.

Later development beyond the Millennium spaces is being carried out by others to a different plan but the relationships of the key spaces have been maintained.

The project for the development of Broad Quay was an opportunity to explore a high density mixed use scheme in a key city centre location, very much in line with the then recently published Richard Roger's Urban Taskforce report.

We proposed to replace the existing tower by a new slightly taller and more complex tower, carefully located off the axis of view past the cathedral, and marking a key historic point of entry into the city. Containing a range of apartments, the tower design responded to the different edge conditions, to views from surrounding streets and to orientation. The lower levels contained offices and further residential, all located over new shops and form new street edges. These elevations established a new urban context.

The whole would have brought a new level of life activity and cohesion to this part of the city, but was not finally to be built.

Our engagement with a major extension to the post war Broadmead shopping area was a different challenge, but with similar priorities. We gave urban design input to the overall masterplan prepared by Chapman Taylor, encouraging pedestrian and visual links into the surrounding network of streets and spaces around and encouraging the principals of openness.

We then concentrated on proposals around the retained historic buildings of Quakers Friars in order to bring new life to a previously rundown area. A gently curved street provides a key link between the older shopping area and the covered parts of Cabot Circus and the Listed buildings were integrated into a new civic square of shops and restaurants with residential above, and the historic buildings were converted into a restaurant and function rooms. The new buildings providing the new setting for these buildings have a scale, form and materials which complement them whilst creating a new and well used public place. The adjacent residential tower rising from a plinth of housing and retail is appropriately of different forms and materials.

The opportunities to design pieces of urban fabric as well as individual buildings have been rewarding.

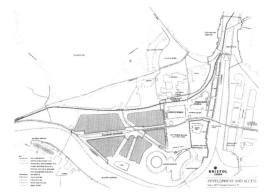

Canon's Marsh, Bristol

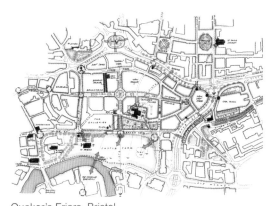

Quaker's Friars, Bristol

Broad Quay

Harbourside Masterplan Bristol 1996

Since the final closure of the city docks to commercial traffic in 1967 the area of railway sidings, dockyard sheds and largely abandoned gas works, known as Canon's Marsh, had remained largely derelict.

Various redevelopments had been attempted but either rejected as unsuitable or abandoned in several recessions. In 1995, Bristol's planning officers were once more developing new guidance for the area and it was agreed that the process would be best taken forward in partnership with the Bristol Initiative. The Bristol Initiative is a private, public and voluntary sector body set up by a group of far sighted business people working closely with local politicians and other key players. It initiates and supports work which will be of benefit to the whole community and has been very effective. The two bodies agreed that the immediate aim should be an overall masterplan which would be the basis for a high quality mixed use development on what was increasingly seen as a valuable and important site in the context of the city as a whole.

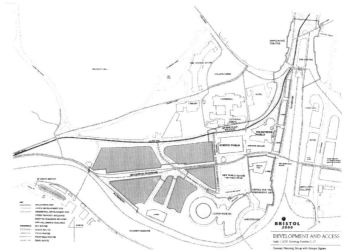

extent of Masterplan

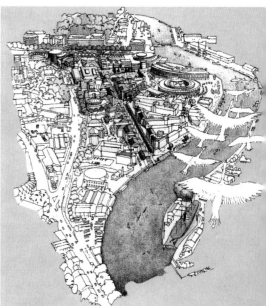

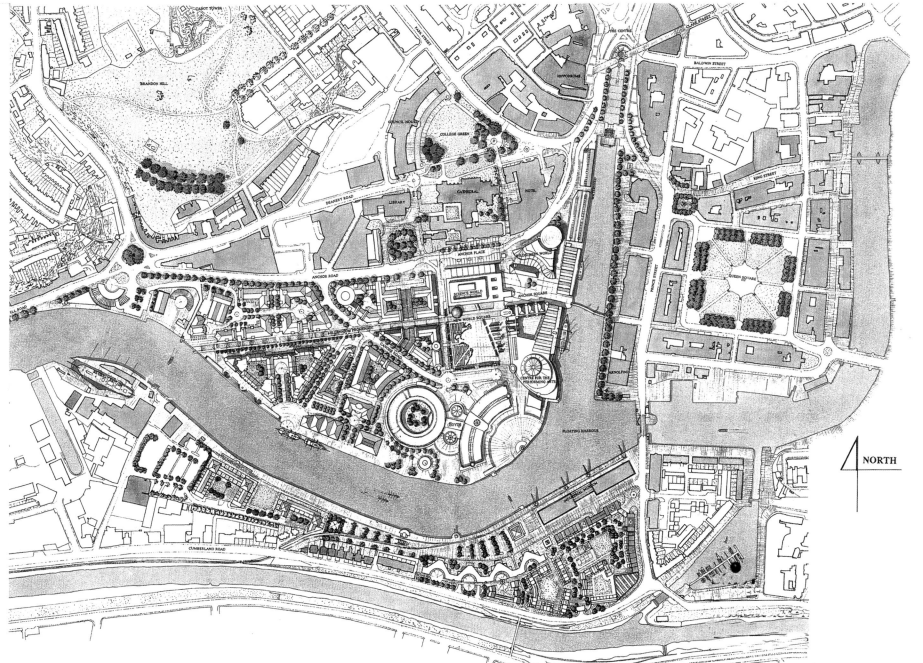

NORTH

A group of four Bristol-based architects, James Bruges, George Ferguson, Richard Lee and David Mellor, were asked by the Initiative to develop planning guidance with the local authority, covering overall strategy, potential mix of uses, key building heights and views. Later the client body also included all the landowners who had been brought together by the local authority. The masterplan envisaged a fairly dense grain of courtyard based development linked to both the water and to a strong east-west axis, soon to become known as Brunel Mile, linking Temple Meads station to the ss *Great Britain*. The courtyards were designed to be residential, office and other uses with a clear hierarchy of public street edges and more private interior courts. Primary routes were to be enlivened with shops and cafes and vehicular movement limited.

Studies showed that the disused GWR railway goods shed, built in 1904 using the then innovative Hennebique form of concrete construction, could adapt well to a

museum type activity. Other buildings to be preserved were the listed Victorian lead-works and gas works buildings. Bristol Cathedral is prominent above the site on its escarpment and axial views of this were built into the plan. The plans received wide public approval.

In parallel, moves were afoot to make a major bid to the Millennium Commission to fund major new visitor attractions and new public squares and the masterplan was to form a crucial part of the bid. The plan was developed to incorporate the emerging new building designs proposed for a hands-on Science Centre in the restored goods shed, and for a Centre for the Natural World and its ecology and a new IMAX theatre incorporating the former Leadworks. A two-level car park for 500 cars was envisaged underneath a major new public square to serve both the new visitor attractions and a proposed Centre for the Performing Arts.

At this stage Richard Lee had been commissioned by Bristol's Leisure Services to develop a 'Brief for Action' study for a major new Centre for the Performing Arts for Bristol, to be located on a key site the

masterplan had identified on the edge of the harbour. This study considered the feasibility of locating a large volume building on this prominent waterfront site. The conclusions were very positive, confirming the demonstrable need for a CPA in Bristol and support for an iconic building in this location. A specific proposal was developed as an option and illustrated on the masterplan submitted to the Millennium Commission. A later international architectural competition for the Centre in which we teamed up with Barton Myers from Los Angeles produced a winning proposal by Stefan Behnisch. Regrettably the final funding for this was not eventually forthcoming but the site remains available for a future key building.

The existence of a coherent masterplan for the whole of Canon's Marsh proved to be key in persuading the Millennium Commission to provide significant funding for a new science and arts quarter for the city.

With public money invested, the private sector could then be encouraged to invest in the development of the rest of the site. A revised masterplan was later drawn up by others.

George Ferguson, James Bruges, Richard Lee, David Mellor

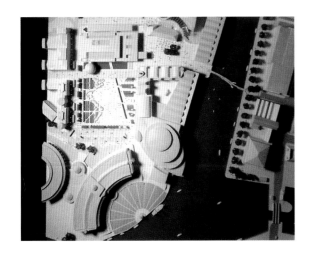

Having established the overall masterplan, Richard Lee and David Mellor together with George Ferguson had worked with the body, then known as Bristol 2000, to bid to the Millennium Commission for a major city centre Millennium project. Most Millennium Commission projects were outside city centres and part of the case to them was the existence of a masterplan showing how the injection of public funds into new, city centre, visitor attractions could help regenerate the whole of a largely derelict area.

In order to compete for the design of the Open Spaces we decided to re-form Concept Planning Group (a body earlier set up by George Ferguson and James Bruges), to include Alec French Architects. It was as CPG that we won the competition for the squares and spaces which were to include a two storey underground car park and associated small buildings.

We also helped facilitate architectural competitions for the hands-on science centre and the natural history centre. These were won respectively by Chris Wilkinson and Michael Hopkins.

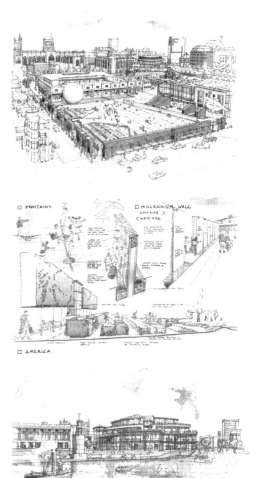

136

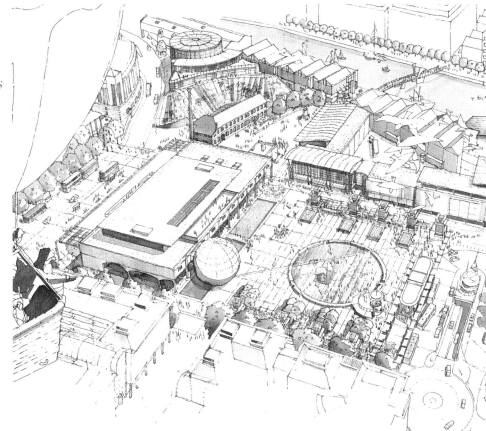

For the submission to the Millennium Commission we worked with a highly innovative and well-respected French landscape architect – Alain Provost of Group Signes. We had seen and admired his work in Paris including Parc Citroen where he used landscape elements as integrated works of art. He undoubtedly helped us to win the funds but his ideas proved a little too radical for the client to be taken beyond bid stage. We then worked with Michael Balston and a range of artists, as explained below, on the final proposals.

A major public square was a key component of our earlier masterplan and in discussion with the client it was clear that this should be a largely paved square suitable for a wide range of events and activities – complementing the grassed College Green and the about to be restored Queen Square. The brief was 'a place for both celebration and contemplation'. As a millennium project the client body, led by its inspirational Chair, Nicholas Hood, was looking for public spaces which would look as good in 100 years as they did on completion. We were expected to use high quality materials such as the hard French limestone paving, used for its colour, texture and durability and the terracotta tiles of the ventilation towers.

The main square is above a two-storey car park requiring high levels of mechanical ventilation. We needed this to be an effectively silent operation and the ventilation towers incorporate considerable acoustic baffling. They were clearly going to be significant elements and were conceived rather in the manner of the trees which surround major historic squares – defining and giving scale to the inner square.

In addition to the main paved area we provided more intimate seating areas interspersed with soft landscaping. Water was always to be a part of the space and a reflecting pool in front of the Science Centre was agreed with Chris Wilkinson. William Pye won the limited competition for a water feature – Aquarena – and we worked closely with him to make this an integral part of the space. Shallow water trickles over bronze steps and cascades down stainless steel. An intriguing analemma-based light sculpture – Zenith by David Ward – uses helicopter landing lights which appear to hover above the surface, and are switched on and off in an unpredictable sequence. All these features are much enjoyed by children and their families. The work of other artists was also integrated into the overall project.

The underground car park was designed to feel light, elegant and generous in use. The stairs up to the square are open to daylight and exit into glass enclosures under curved painted roofs. This avoids the usual enclosed feel of such stairs and also provides good orientation as you emerge.

It was also a major engineering feat, developed with Arups. Being built into very wet clay it had to be restrained from floating and was built from the top down. Welded sheet piles provide the enclosure.

Anchor Square is defined by the restored Victorian leadworks, converted to a restaurant with offices over, by South Building (see opposite) and by the west end of the science centre. We largely reused the existing granite setts and retained a cast iron weighbridge, but we also used new paving to provide easily accessible routes across the space. A line of pear trees adds softness and scale.

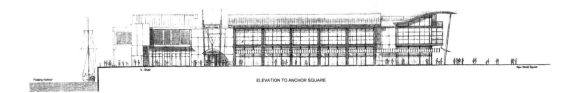

ELEVATION TO ANCHOR SQUARE

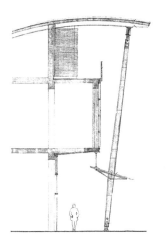

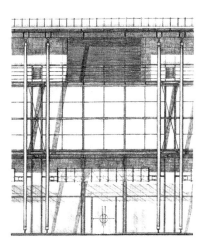

In parallel with the millennium work the practice was commissioned by the JT Group to develop a key corner site which defines both one side of the newly-created Anchor Square and also the corner of Millennium Square. This leisure use building, known as South Building, uses 12-metre laminated 'masts', giving scale and rhythm to a form which responds in its section to the different scales of the two spaces.

Illustration by Richard Carman

Part of the successful case to the Millennium Commission was that the 'Centre' (so called as it had been the central interchange of the tramway system) needed significant enhancement as the gateway to the new Millennium buildings and spaces.

This area had for many years been a four-lane traffic gyratory offering no civic space of any quality and dominated by vehicles.

The plan removed traffic from the southern end allowing a new relationship with the floating harbour celebrated by a cascade, places to sit and new ferry pontoons.

The eastern edge is restricted to buses and the central area widened to allow for seating, trees and other soft landscaping and fountains between areas of timber decking. The sound of the water jets help to offsett the noise of the remaining traffic on the western edge. A series of illuminated beacons by Martin Richman add colour and interest by night.

Quakers Friars Bristol 2009

In 2000 a developer competition for the eastern expansion of Broadmead shopping centre was won by Land Securities who teamed up with Hammerson to form The Bristol Alliance. This very significant investment in Bristol, involving major site clearance and the diversion of the inner ring road, aimed to transform the city's retail strength.

AFA's initial role in supporting the lead architects, Chapman Taylor, was to identify urban design issues generally and assist with public consultation in particular. The Bristol Alliance then appointed AFA as concept architects for the area known as Quakers Friars. This involved both significant work to listed buildings and new residential and retail.

If in the past you had mentioned the name 'Quakers Friars' to Bristolians they would have associated it with a backwater of Broadmead shopping centre where a group of old buildings gave a home to the Bristol Registry Office surrounded by car parking and service yards. Yet this is one of the most precious historical groups of buildings left standing in Bristol today. Two medieval halls, Cutlers and Bakers, and a Victorian link building are what remains of a Dominican Friary founded by Maurice de Gault in 1228, and are rare examples of thirteenth-century monastic architecture,

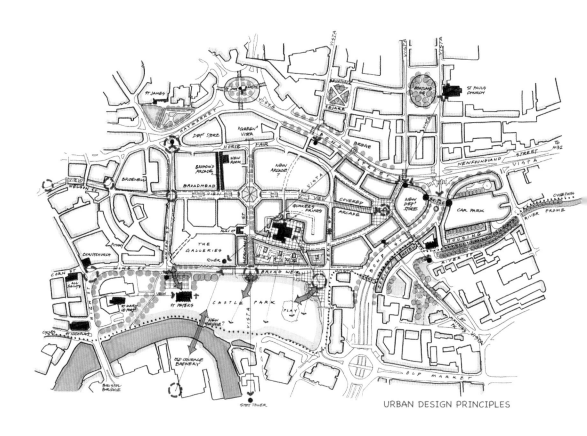

URBAN DESIGN PRINCIPLES

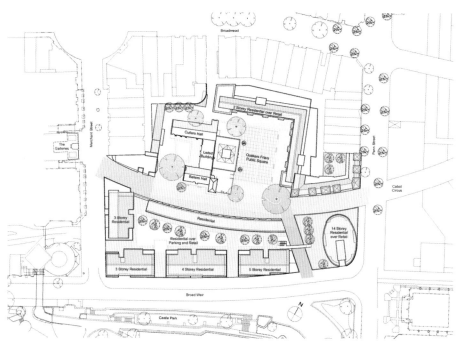

Quakers Friars in its new setting

Residential above retail

1747 Quakers Meeting

Quakers Meeting interior

including some of the oldest timber roofs in Bristol. The focus of this group of listed buildings remains the 1747 Quakers Meeting Room by George and William Tulley. The site had been acquired by the Society of Friends in about 1670 in whose ownership it remained until sold to Bristol City Council in 1955. It became clear that a viable use had to be found for this *queer group of buildings* as Pevsner called it.

These listed buildings posed an interesting challenge for the developer and the architect as their reuse demanded a successful commercial use and significant expenditure in restoring the buildings to their former glory. Finding an appropriate use as a high class restaurant in the Quakers Meeting Room, together with function rooms in the medieval halls, was well received by the public who now recognise the historic gem that is Quakers Friars.

At the heart of the new Quakers Friars area is a public square which is formed by screening the back of the existing shops in Broadmead with new, three-storey retail and residential buildings. The square is of a scale that sits comfortably with the setting of the Listed Buildings and engages with the curved street that leads to Cabot Circus (the new covered mall area) to the east and the pre existing Galleries Centre to the west. The square contains areas of seating, fountains and soft landscaping to make this a welcoming space and place to relax and enjoy al fresco eating, drinking and outside performance. The proposals ensured that a prominent plane tree survived the redevelopment process and contributes greatly to the environment. The surrounding buildings are varied in character but conforming to an

overall aesthetic appropriately forming a background to the square. The transformation of this area has been much appreciated by those who knew the old Quakers Friars.

Working closely with the planning authority and English Heritage we agreed a massing for the new development that increased in scale from three storeys around the public square stepping up to five storeys on Broad Weir overlooking Castle Park and culminating in a 17-storey tower on the corner of Penn Street and Broad Weir. In all cases residential is provided above retail. The tower includes a three-storey retail podium, currently occupied by Harvey Nichols, with roof garden and bridge link to car parking.

This new addition to the Bristol skyline has a distinctive oval form with recessed balconies. It can be seen from much of the city, its silver skin glinting in the light.

Continuity

Practices benefit from continuity as well as new blood and new ideas. In the 1970s Richard and David inherited an ethos and reputation of a well-established, Bristol-based practice set up in the 1920s building on its strength and moving it onwards. Nigel Dyke and Mark Osborne are now doing the same.

Nigel and Mark have been Directors since 2002. Both of them have played key roles in many of the buildings illustrated in the earlier sections, but have also been responsible for their own projects, some of which are illustrated in the following pages. They are bringing their own creativity and innovation to the practice whilst continuing to explore many of the themes that have been discussed.

For the past thirty years the practice has enjoyed a wide spread of work, of varying scale, in both public and private sectors and remains committed to this range of work.

The practice continues to make well designed, sustainable and appropriate architecture – providing our clients with solutions that meet both their needs and their aspirations.

Mark Osborne   Nigel Dyke   David Mellor   Richard Lee

Education: City Learning Centre, Whitefield School, Bristol 2003

This City learning Centre serving is located at the Whitefield Community School. This has a particular emphasis on inclusiveness for the many ethnic communities served by the school and for children with learning difficulties. As well as ICT teaching rooms, there is a central dance and performance space and a sound room. The learning spaces are separated from this area by large sliding/folding screens that enable great flexibility in arrangement and size of spaces for different class sizes and activities.

Residential: Woodland Court, Bristol 2005

Woodland Court provides 200 study bedrooms for the University of Bristol. The bedrooms are arranged in flats for up to six students, each with a communal kitchen and dining area. Most are in new blocks around paved courtyards and the rest in the adjacent, nineteenth century refurbished Woodland House. The scale and the massing of the new accommodation was determined by the grain of the surrounding Victorian villas and terraces, with the buildings designed to be sympathetic to their context, whilst retaining their own integrity. There is a striking stainless steel courtyard gate by artist John Packer.

Offices: Tower Wharf, Bristol 2006

The new offices are situated on the edge of Bristol's Floating Harbour and immediately adjacent to the Grade II Listed Lead Shot Tower. The scheme provides 7,850m² of high quality open plan office accommodation on six floors, over semi-basement car parking. The building has a dramatic entrance atrium linking the primary floors. There are balconies overlooking the harbour and the top two floors are stepped back on the west elevation to provide external terrace areas with views over the city. A waterfront colonnade along the harbour edge is incorporated into the building at ground level, enriched by steel screens created by the artist John Packer. Access to a new ferry landing is also provided. Tower Wharf achieved an Excellent BREEAM rating.

Community: Netham Park Pavilion, Bristol 2007

This new community building is designed to be the centre piece and catalyst for the regeneration of Netham Park in Bristol. The content of the building was a result of extensive local consultation. The new sports, community, and park rangers' building is on two levels with the lower level partially buried into the existing sloping site. Changing rooms are on the lower level directly accessing the sports pitches. The community room and cafe on the upper level address the main park. The building is highly sustainable and heating is by a biomass boiler.

Education: Faculty of Art, Media & Design, UWE, Bristol 2008

Planning consent was gained for a 10 year masterplan to reorganise and refurbish the Bower Ashton campus, replacing redundant buildings. The first phase involved a new reception, administration, IT and studio building at a new entrance position to the campus. The exhibition gallery, supported on mushroom columns, is skewed in plan to address a pathway through the woods. The main body of the building stretches out alongside the woods and is clad in larch, with tilted planks above picture windows to allow discrete natural ventilation. Patinated copper cladding accentuates projecting elements such as the angular north lights to first floor studios. Once completed, the second phase of full refurbishment of the main teaching block could begin.

Offices: Deanery Road, Bristol 2010

With Westmark Developments, we were selected in competition by Bristol City Council for the redevelopment of this key inner city site, close to the Council House, the Central Library and Brunel House. The mixed use proposals contain two office buildings of 8,000m^2 and 3,125m^2, 78 apartments (including 23 affordable) a retail unit, car parking and a new public square. The design creates a street frontage of varying character to Deanery Road, interspersed with front entrances to the various buildings.

The Environment Agency has chosen the main office component as their new national headquarters. This building is the winner of the BREEAM Award 2010 for highest rated office building in the UK. The building performs well over all of the BREEAM categories. Key components are the mixed mode ventilation system, the ground source heat pumps and the use of sustainable and accredited materials.

Education, Briarwood Special Needs School, Bristol – on-going

Briarwood Special Needs School has a wide catchment area, providing education for 80 children and young people between the ages of 3 and19. This proposal brings the currently fragmented nursery, primary and sixth form elements to the secondary school site to enable the school to function more effectively. Developing the brief included extensive consultation with BCC and senior staff. The new school building completes a trio of very different buildings, the existing secondary school, our former CLC building which will be incorporated and the new primary building. The simple timber cladding on the new, single storey building is approachable and calm whilst the rooftop cubes are a vibrant architectural expression of the ventilation strategy. This new building forms two court-yards, one with extensive imaginative interventions for boisterous play and the other a more secluded, peaceful sensory garden.

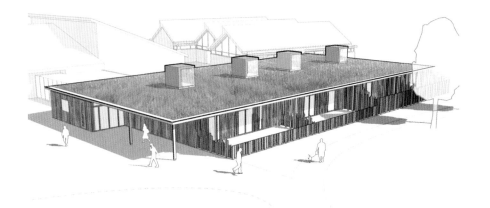

Kingswood Locality Hub, South Gloucestershire – on-going

This new Children and Young Persons Locality Hub is a joint venture between the Council, the Primary Care Trust and the North Bristol Trust. The new building will bring together a wide range of key services in an accessible and uplifting environment. The building is constructed of solid timber giving excellent sustainability credentials. Completion will be in 2011.

Education: Abbeywood Community School, Filton, Gloucestershire 2010

This school for 1260 pupils incorporates shared learning spaces and extensive external teaching spaces arranged around a curved internal 'street' also used for dining. The pattern of coloured glass in the central roof light was design by the tudents. It is highly sustainable, benefiting from high thermal mass, natural ventilation, good daylighting and passive solar gain. It also incorporates a biomass boiler, solar hot water collection and photo-voltaic cells.

Mixed use: Redcliffe Wharf, Bristol – on-going

This is a very sensitive site being one of the few undeveloped quaysides, containing active boat building and being on key views of St. Mary Redcliffe church. The development brief emerged from a collaboration with the local Redcliffe Futures Group and Bristol City Council as both landowners and planning authority, and was presented as a three dimensional planning brief. The new buildings provide for a mix of residential office and leisure uses. The existing boat building yard is to be re-housed on the site. New public spaces are provided for a variety of uses and key views are maintained.

Housing: 78-100, St Michaels Hill, Bristol

Client:	Special Trustees Hospital Board
Completed:	1980
AFA:	Michael Collings, Richard Lee, Charles Gregory

Offices: The Grove, Bristol

Client:	Standard Life
Completed:	1980
AFA:	Michael Collings, Richard Lee, Tony Clarke

Offices: Broad Quay House, Bristol

Completed:	1981
AFA:	Ian Thornton, Richard Lee, Helena Durrant, Roger Foster, John Hartnell, Bill Jacques, Richard Silverman
Structure:	Clarke Nicholls & Marcel
Services:	Ferguson and Partners
QS:	Gleeds

Offices: Narrow Quay House, Bristol

Client:	Standard Life
Completed:	1981
AFA:	Richard Lee, Henry Alpass
Structure:	Clarke Nicholls & Marcel
Services:	Ferguson and Partners
QS:	Gleeds

Retail: Old Market Centre, Taunton

Client:	Standard Life
Completed:	1982
AFA:	Michael Collings, Richard Lee, David Ricks, Charles Gregory
Structure:	Clark Nichols & Marcell
Services:	Ferguson & Partners
QS:	Gleeds

Residential: Buchanans Wharf Competition

Competition:	1982
AFA:	Richard Lee, Edward Nash

Retail: St Marys Centre, Thornbury, South Gloucestershire

Client:	Grosvenor Estate
Completed:	1983
AFA:	David Mellor, Ian Stevenson
QS:	Gleeds

Retail: New Broadmead, Bristol

Client:	Bristol United Press
Completed:	1984
AFA:	Michael Collings, David Mel David Ricks
Structure:	John Farquharson
QS:	Gleeds

Offices: Brunel House, Bristol

Client:	CIS
Completed:	1984
AFA:	Richard Lee, Roger Guck, Adrian Jones

Salvation Army Citadel, Ashley Road, Bristol

Client:	Salvation Army
Completed:	1987
AFA:	David Mellor, John Fjeld
Structure:	Curtins

Offices: Narrow Lewins, Bristol

Client:	Haslemere Estates
Completed:	1985
AFA:	Richard Lee, Henry Alpass, David Kent
Structure:	Arup
Services:	Hoare Lea & Partners
QS:	Gleeds

Retail: Gammon Lane, Barnstaple

Client:	Rosehaugh Heritage
Completed:	1988
AFA:	Richard Lee, Charles Gregory

Manufacturing: Sas Factory Bridgend

Client:	SAS
Completed:	1986
AFA:	David Mellor, Henry Alpass
Structure:	Clarke Bond
QS:	Davis Langdon

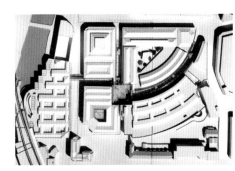

Retail: Southgate Street, Bath

Client:	Prudential Portfolio Managers
Un-built Project:	1986-1989
AFA:	Michael Collings, David Mellor, Alison Bell, Nigel Honer

Offices: No. 1, Bridewell Street, Bristol

Client:	MEPC
Completed:	1987
AFA:	Richard Lee, Richard Silverman, David Ricks, Roger Guck
Structure:	Clarke Bond
Services:	WS Atkins
QS:	Banks Wood

Offices: 4/5 Portwall Lane, Bristol

Client:	MEPC
Completed:	1990
AFA:	Richard Lee, John Fjeld, Alan Quick
Structure:	Clarke Bond
Services:	BSDC
QS:	Banks Wood

Education: King Edwards School, Bath

Client:	King Edward's School
Completed:	1990
AFA:	David Mellor, Keith Boxer
Structure:	Arup
Services:	Hoare Lea & Partners
QS:	Gleeds

Offices: Redcliff Quay, Bristol

Client:	Standard Life
Completed:	1991
AFA:	Richard Lee, David Ricks, Dav Kent, Glen Gareis
Structure:	Arup
Services:	Hoare Lea & Partners
QS:	Gleeds

see page

Offices: 33-35 Queen Square, Bristol

Client:	Refuge Assurance
Completed:	1990
AFA:	David Mellor, Huw James, Neil Stacey
Structure:	Peter Goodhind Associates
Services:	BSDC
QS:	Faithful and Gould

Offices: Castlewood, Clevedon

Client:	Clerical Medical Investment G
Completed:	1992
AFA:	Michael Collings, Richard Lee Charles Gregory, Simon Lawr Carol Carey, Roger Guck
Structure:	Arup
Services:	Hoare Lea & Partners
QS:	Gleeds

Offices: 31 Great George St, Bristol

Client:	Philip Mero / Church Commissioners for England
Completed:	1990
AFA:	David Mellor, Richard Lee, Mark Osborne, Carol Carey, Chris Mitchell
Structure:	TM Ventham
Services:	Hoare Lea & Partners
QS:	Gordon Harris

St Anne's College, Oxford

Client:	St Anne's College
Completed:	1992
AFA:	Richard Lee, David Mellor, G Davis, Ruth Neilsen
Structure:	Kenneth Brown & Partners
Services:	WSP Parsons Brown
QS:	Gleeds

Offices: Manley House, Exeter

Client:	National Rivers Authority
Completed:	1990
AFA:	Richard Lee, John Fjeld, Carol Carey
Structure:	Roughton & Fenton
Services:	Hoare Lea & Partners
QS:	Gleeds

Offices: St Georges Road, Bristol

Client:	Pentagon
Un-Built Project:	1992
AFA:	Richard Lee, John Fjeld, Sim Lawrence, Andrew Brown

Centre for the Visually Impaired, Bristol

Client:	Bristol Royal Society for the Blind
Completed:	1993
AFA:	Richard Lee, John Fjeld, Helen Hollis, Chris Mitchell
Structure:	Kenneth Brown & Partners
Services:	WSP
QS:	Colin Jenkins

Retail: Yate, South Gloucestershire

Client:	MEPC
Completed:	1993
AFA:	David Mellor, Chris Mitchell, John Fjeld, Carol Carey
Structure:	John Farquharson
Services:	Hoare Lea & Partners
QS:	Gleeds

Marketing and Visitor Centre, Bristol

Client:	Bristol Development Corporation
	Winner of limited competition
Completed:	1993
AFA:	David Mellor, Nigel Widdup
Structure:	Whitby Bird (Mark Lovell)
Services:	Whitby Bird
QS:	James Nisbet

Student Accommodation: Goldney Hall, Bristol

Client:	University of Bristol
	Winner of limited competition
Completed:	1994
AFA:	David Mellor, Mark Osborne, Huw James
Structure:	Whitby Bird
Services:	Whitby Bird
QS:	Gleeds
Landscape:	Balston

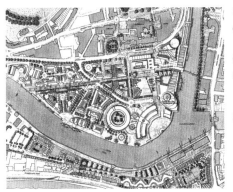

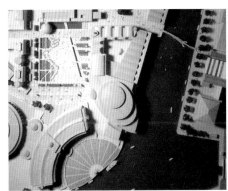

Master planning, Harbourside, Bristol

Client:	Harbourside Landowners Group
Completed:	1996
Concept Planning Group	(AFA with Ferguson Mann Architects)
CPG:	James Bruges, George Ferguson, Richard Lee, David Mellor, David Caird, Mark Osborne

University of Bath Library extension

Client:	University of Bath
	Winner of limited competition
Completed:	1996
AFA:	Richard Lee, David Ricks, Tim Must
Structure:	Oscar Faber
Services:	Oscar Faber
QS:	James Nisbet

Centre for Performing Arts Study: Bristol

Client:	Bristol City Council
Completed:	1996
AFA:	Richard Lee
Theatre Consultants:	Carr and Angier

Offices: Venturers House, Bristol

Client:	Helical Bar
Completed:	1996
AFA:	David Mellor, John Fjeld, Mark Osborne
Structure:	Ernest Green
Services:	Hilson Moran
QS:	Bucknall Austin

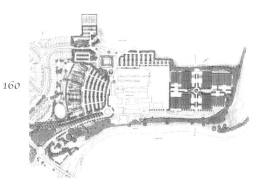

Masterplanning: Cadbury's Site, Keynsham

Client:	Cadburys
Project:	1997
AFA:	Richard Lee
Landscape:	Novell Tullett

Urban design: Millennium Spaces, Bristol

Client:	At-Bristol
	Winner of limited competition
Completed:	2000
	As Concept Planning Group AFA with Ferguson Mann Architects
CPG:	David Mellor, George Ferguso David Caird
Structure :	Arup
Services :	Arup
QS:	Symonds

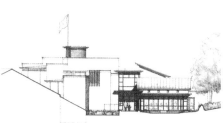

Arts: The Invasion Centre, Fishguard

Client:	Invasion Centre committee
Winner of limited competition 1998	
Un-built Project	
AFA:	David Mellor, Huw James, Neil Stacey

Car Park: Millennium Square, Bristol

Client:	At-Bristol
Completed:	2000
	As Concept Planning Group AFA with Ferguson Mann Architects
CPG:	David Mellor, David Ricks
Structure:	Arup
Services:	Arup
QS:	Symonds

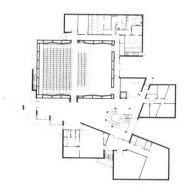

Education: Arts & Media Centre, Stourbridge

Client:	Ridgewood School
Winner of limited competition 1998	
Un-built Project	
AFA:	David Mellor, Huw James, Carol Carey
Structure:	Mark Lovell Design

Urban Design: The Centre, Bristol

Client:	Bristol City Council
Completed:	2000
	As Concept Planning Group AFA with Ferguson Mann Architects
CPG:	George Ferguson, David Mel Mark Osborne, Liz Davis
Structure:	Bristol City Council
QS:	Davis Langdon

Manufacturing: Latchways plc, Devizes

Client:	Latchways plc
Completed:	1999
AFA:	Richard Lee, John Fjeld, David Ricks
Structure:	Structures One
Services:	BS Solutions
QS:	Gardiner & Theobald

Low-energy housing: Bishop Sutton, Somer

Client:	Edward Ware New Homes
Un-built Project	2000
AFA:	Richard Lee, Ray Lambe

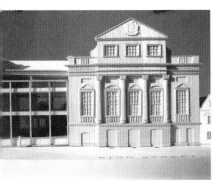

Consultancy, Theatre Royal, Bristol

Client:	Bristol Old Vic Trustees
	1980-1990
AFA:	R Lee, John Fjeld, Carol Carey
Historic Building:	Donald Insall & Partners
Theatre:	Carr and Angier
Auditorium:	Michael Forsyth
QS:	Gleeds

Education, City Learning Centres Bristol

Client:	Bristol City Council
Completed:	2001
AFA:	David Mellor, Nigel Dyke, Oliver Grimshaw
Structure:	Whicheloe MacFarlane
Services:	Whicheloe MacFarlane
QS:	Northcroft

Student accommodation: 1 St Georges Road, Bristol

Client:	Acton Housing Association
Completed:	2001
AFA:	David Mellor, John Fjeld, Tom Russell, Spencer Back
Structure:	Clarke Bond
Services:	Ryan Associates
QS:	Gleeds

Mixed Use, Broad Quay Site, Bristol

Client:	Grosvenor Development
Un-built Project	1999-2002
AFA:	David Mellor, Mark Osborne, Tom Russell, Jon Chadwick
Structure:	Buro Happold
Services:	Buro Happold
QS:	EC Harris

Leisure: South Building, Bristol

Client:	John Pontin, JT Group
Completed:	2001
AFA:	Richard Lee, Huw James, Neil Stacey

Capricorn Quay, Harbourside, Bristol

Client:	Beaufort / Crosby Homes
Completed:	2002
AFA:	Richard Lee, Huw James, John Fjeld
Structure:	Clarke Bond
Services:	Mitie
QS:	Gleeds

New Faculty of Education, UWE, Bristol

Client:	University of the West of England
	Winner of limited competition
Completed:	2001
AFA:	Richard Lee, Mark Osborne, John Fjeld, Liz Davis, Carol Carey
Structure:	Arup
Services:	BJP Consulting
QS:	Gleeds
Landscape:	Cooper Partnership

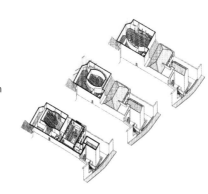

Jewish Arts and Heritage Centre, Bristol

Client:	Bristol Hebrew Congregation
Un-built Project	2003
AFA:	Richard Lee, John Fjeld,
Structure:	Kenneth Brown & Partners
Services:	Hoare Lea & Partners
QS:	Gleeds

Education: City Learning Centre, Whitefield School, Bristol

Client:	Bristol City Council
Completed:	2003
AFA:	Nigel Dyke, Matt Harrison
Structure:	Arup
Services:	Arup
QS:	Ridge

Offices: Tower Wharf, Bristol

Client:	HBG Properties
Completed:	2006
AFA:	Mark Osborne, Nigel Rayne, Joy Stone, James Aplin
Structure:	Buro Happold
Services:	Hoare Lea & Partners

Conference Centre: Sheepdrove Farm, Berkshire

Client:	Peter and Juliet Kindersley
Completed:	2005
AFA:	David Mellor, Nigel Dyke, Matt Harrison, Tom Russell
Structure:	Mark Lovell Design
Services:	Halcrow
QS:	Gleeds

ss *Great Britain*, Bristol

Client:	The Trustees
Completed:	2006
AFA:	David Mellor, John Fjeld, Tim Burgess
Structure:	Arup and Fenton Holloway
Services:	WSP
QS:	Symonds

Student Accommodation: Woodland Court, Bristol

Client:	Acton Housing Association
Completed:	2005
AFA:	Mark Osborne, John Fjeld, Gayle Stevens
Structure:	Engage Consult
Services:	Star
QS:	Gleeds

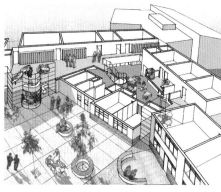
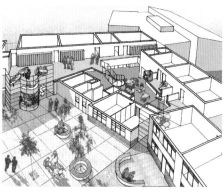

Education: Brislington School, Bristol

Client:	BAM / Bristol City Council PFI competition
Un-built Project	2006
AFA:	David Mellor, Zac Nicholson, Kasia Freyer, Joy Stone
Structure:	Arup
Services:	Arup
QS:	Gardiner & Theobald

Education: Henbury School, Bristol

Client:	BAM / Bristol City Council
Completed:	2005
AFA:	David Mellor, Nigel Dyke, Tamsin Thomas, Liz Davis, Joy Stone
Structure:	Arup
Services:	Arup
QS:	Gardiner & Theobald

Education: Monks Park School, Bristol

Client:	BAM/ Bristol City Council
Completed:	2006
AFA:	Nigel Dyke, Toby Jefferies, Louise Ciotti
Structure:	Arup
Services:	Arup
QS:	Gardiner & Theobald

Penny Brohn Cancer Care Centre, Pill, N. Somerset

Client:	The Trustees
Completed:	2007
AFA:	Richard Lee, John Fjeld, Liz Davis
	Nigel Rayner, Tamsin Thomas
Structure:	Mark Lovell Design
Services:	Hoare Lea & Partners

Healthy buildings consultant: Dr David Crowther

Project management: Andrew Wilson

Community: Visitor Centre, Monmouth

163

Client:	Monmouthshire County Council
	Winner of limited competition
Un-built Project	2006-2008
AFA:	Nigel Dyke, Gayle Stevens
Structure:	Structures 1
Services:	BDP
QS:	Gardiner & Theobald
Landscape:	Novell Tullett

Leisure: ss *Great Britain* Café, Bristol

Client:	The Trustees
Completed:	2007
AFA:	David Mellor, Toby Jefferies, Gayle Stevens

22-25 Queen Square, Bristol

Client:	Westmark
Completed:	2008
AFA:	Mark Osborne, Richard Lee, Zac Nicholson, Jon Chadwick
Structure:	Buro Happold
Services:	Hoare Lea & Partners
Historic Building Consultant:	Donald Insall

Community: Netham Pavilion, Bristol

Client:	Bristol City Council
Completed:	2007
AFA:	Nigel Dyke, Joy Stone, Tamsin Thomas
Structure:	Integral Structural Design
Services:	Building Services Solutions
QS:	Peter Ballingall

Faculty of Art, Media & Design, Bristol

Client:	UWE
Completed:	2008
AFA:	Mark Osborne, Nick Vaughan, Liz Davis, Kasia Freyer, Joy Stone
Structure:	Arup
Services:	Hoare Lea & Partners
QS:	Currie & Brown
Landscape:	Cooper Partnership

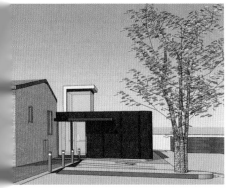

Community: Black Development Agency, Bristol

Client:	Black Development Agency
Un-built Project	2007
AFA:	Nigel Dyke, Joy Stone, Jon Chadwick
Structure:	Structures 1
Services:	BDP
QS:	Gardiner & Theobald

Residential: John Foster's Almshouse, Bristol

Client:	Bristol Charities
Completed:	2008
AFA:	Richard Lee, Nigel Dyke, Nigel Rayner, Gayle Stevens, Jonathan Davey
Structure:	Structures 1
Services:	Building Services Solutions
QS:	Hugh Whatley

Offices: Aardman Animations HQ, Bristol

Client:	Aardman Animations
Completed:	2009
AFA:	David Mellor, Nick Vaughan, Kasia Freyer, Jenny Gossage, Simon Rayner, Tamsin Thomas
Structure:	Arup, Mark Lovell (staircase)
Services:	Arup
QS:	Gleeds

Somerset College of Art & Technology

Client:	Somerset College
	Winner of limited competition
Un-built Project	2008-2009
AFA:	Mark Osborne, Robin Gray, Gayle Stevens
Structure:	Ramboll Whitby Bird
Services:	WSP
QS:	Turner Townsend

Refurbishment: Quakers Friars, Bristol

Client:	The Bristol Alliance
Completed:	2009
AFA:	Richard Lee, Nigel Dyke, David Ricks, Barbara Hicks
Structure:	Watermans
Services:	Hoare Lea & Partners
Conservation architect: Philip Hughes	
QS:	Cyril Sweett

Offices and residential: Deanery Road, Bristol

Client:	Westmark
Completed:	2010
AFA:	Mark Osborne, John Fjeld, Chris Colyer, Jonathan Davey, Rob Mills, Zac Nicholson, Nigel Rayner, Simon Rayner, Joy Stone
Structure:	Arup
Services:	Arup / Hoare Lea & Partners
QS:	Northcroft

Mixed Use: Quakers Friars, Bristol

Client:	The Bristol Alliance
Completed:	2009
AFA:	Richard Lee, Nigel Dyke, David Ricks, Tom Russell, Barabara Hicks, Jon Chadwick, Tamsin Thomas, Gayle Stevens
Structure:	Waterman
Services:	Hoare Lea & Partners
QS:	Cyril Sweett

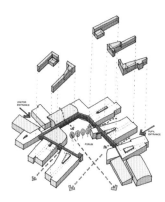

Education: Melksham School, Wiltshire

Client:	Wiltshire County Council
Completed:	2010
AFA:	Nigel Dyke, Zac Nicholson, Joy Stone, Tobias Feilding-Crawley
Structure:	Arup
Services:	Arup
QS:	Gardiner & Theobald

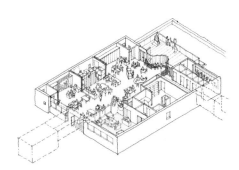

Education: Project Fusion Diploma Centre, Bristol

Client:	At-Bristol
Un-built Project	2009
AFA:	David Mellor, Kasia Freyer

Education: Abbeywood School, Bristol

Client:	South Gloucestershire Council
Completed:	2010
AFA:	Nigel Dyke, David Mellor, Zac Nicholson, Tobias Feilding-Crawley
Structure:	Arup
Services:	Arup
QS:	Gardiner & Theobald

Brunel Institute, ss *Great Britain*, Bristol

Client:	The Trustees
Completed:	2010
AFA:	David Mellor, John Fjeld, Liz Davis, Kasia Freyer, Rob Mills, Nigel Rayner
Structure:	Structures 1
Services:	WSP
QS:	Paul Chappell

Kingswood Locality Hub, Gloucestershire

Client:	South Gloucestershire Council
	On-going
AFA:	Nigel Dyke, Robin Gray, Nick Vaughan, Simon Rayner, Louis Lane
Structure:	Integral Structural Design
Services:	Parsons Brinckerhoff
QS:	Cyril Sweett

Mixed use: Redcliffe Wharf, Bristol

Client:	Westmark
	On-going
AFA:	Mark Osborne, Joy Stone
Structure:	Fenton Holloway/ Mark Lovell Design
Services:	Hoare Lea & Partners
QS:	Cyril Sweett

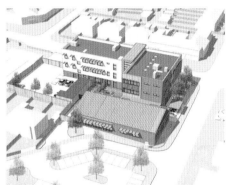

Severnvale Locality Hub, Gloucestershire

Client:	South Gloucestershire Council
	On-going
AFA:	Nigel Dyke, Robin Gray, Zac Nicholson, Elspeth Faulkner
Structure:	Integral Structural Design
Services:	Parsons Brinckerhoff
QS:	Cyril Sweett

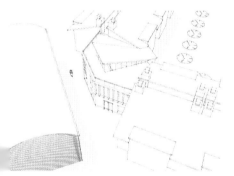

Residential: Sheepdrove Farm, Berkshire

Client:	Peter Kindersley
	On-going
AFA:	David Mellor, Jenny Gossage, Simon Rayner
Structure:	Mark Lovell Design
Services:	Fulcrum Consulting
QS:	Gardiner & Theobald

Education: Briarwood School, Bristol

Client:	Skanska UK/ Bristol CC
	On-going
AFA:	Nigel Dyke, Jenny Gossage, Barbara Hicks
Structure:	Arup
Services:	Jones King

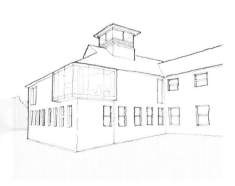

Refurbishment: Kingswood Civic Centre, South Gloucestershire

Client:	South Gloucestershire Council
	On-going
AFA:	Nigel Dyke, Nick Vaughan, Gayle Stevens, Robin Gray
Structure:	Integral Structural Design
Services:	South Gloucestershire Council
QS:	Cyril Sweett

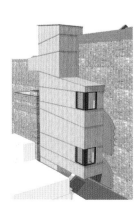

New Facilities: Bristol Museum and Art Gallery

Client:	Bristol City Council
	On-going
AFA:	Nigel Dyke, Jenny Gossage
Structure:	Brunel Design Partnership
Services:	Haughton Greenlees Associates

SELECTED BIBLIOGRAPHY AND AWARDS

AARDMAN ANIMATIONS HEADQUARTERS, BRISTOL 2009

Kursty Groves, *I Wish I Worked There*, March 2010

- RIBA Award
- RIBA Town & Country Design Awards – Workplace and Premier Award
- Bristol Civic Society Award

HORIZON HOUSE, BRISTOL 2010

- BREEAM Offices Award: highest-rated office building in the UK

JOHN FOSTERS ALMSHOUSE, BRISTOL 2010

- The Almshouse Association Patrons Award

QUAKERS FRIARS, BRISTOL 2009

- Bristol Civic Society Award

CABOT CIRCUS/QUAKERS FRIARS, BRISTOL 2009

Michael Jenner, *Bristol's 100 Best Buildings*, 2010

- Supreme Gold Award, British Council of Shopping Centres
- BREEAM Retail Award

FACULTY OF ART, MEDIA AND DESIGN, UWE, BRISTOL 2008

- Bristol Civic Society Award

22-25 QUEEN SQUARE, BRISTOL 2007

- Georgian Group: Best New Building in a Georgian Context

SS *GREAT BRITAIN*, BRISTOL 2006

Architects Journal 16 March 2006

- RIBA Award
- RIBA Crown Estate Conservation Award
- Gulbenkian Museum of the Year
- Civic Trust Award and Special Award for Access

WOODLAND COURT, BRISTOL 2005

- Bristol Civic Society Award

KINDERSLEY CENTRE, SHEEPDROVE FARM, BERKSHIRE 2005

Architects Journal 15 July 2004

Fourth Door Review issue 7 2004

- Civic Trust Award and Special Award for Sustainability

CAPRICORN QUAY, BRISTOL 2002

Tony Aldous, *C20/21 Bristol's Modern Buildings*, 2000

Andrew Foyle, Pevsner Architectural Guides, *Bristol*, 2004

- Bristol Civic Society Award
- National Home Builder Design Commendation

FACULTY OF EDUCATION, UWE, BRISTOL 2001

- Civic Trust Commendation

SOUTH BUILDING, BRISTOL 2001

Architects Journal 12 September 1996

CITY LEARNING CENTRES, BRISTOL 2001

Tony Aldous, *C20/21 Bristol's Modern Buildings*, 2000

- Prime Minister's Award for Better Public Building
- Bristol Civic Society Award

MILLENNIUM SPACES, AT-BRISTOL 2000

Architects Journal 12 September 1996

Building Magazine, 20 March 1998

Building Magazine, 7 July 2000

Tony Aldous, *C20/21 Bristol's Modern Buildings*, 2000

Andrew Foyle, Pevsner Architectural Guides, *Bristol*, 2004

Michael Jenner, *Bristol's 100 Best Buildings*, 2010

- Civic Trust Award and Special Award for Urban Design
- RTPI National Commendation for Planning in the Public Realm
- Bristol Civic Society Award

CAR PARK, AT-BRISTOL 2000

- The British Parking Industry Award

VENTURERS HOUSE, BRISTOL 1996

Architects Journal 12 September 1996

- Bristol Civic Society Award

BATH UNIVERSITY LIBRARY EXTENSION 1996

Architects Journal 12 September 1996

Michael Forsyth, Pevsner Architectural Guides, *Bath*, 2003

- Civic Trust Special Mention
- Structural Steel Award

GOLDNEY HALL, BRISTOL 1994

Architecture Today February 1995

Perspectives, April/May 1996

Tony Aldous, *C20/21 Bristol's Modern Buildings*, 2000

Andrew Foyle, Pevsner Architectural Guides, *Bristol*, 2004

- Civic Trust Commendation
- Bristol Civic Society Award

CENTRE FOR THE VISUALLY IMPAIRED, BRISTOL 1993

Architects Journal 27 October 1993

The Independent 14 April 1993

Tony Aldous, *C20/21 Bristol's Modern Buildings*, 2000

Andrew Foyle, Pevsner Architectural Guides, *Bristol*, 2004

- Bristol Civic Society Award

MARKETING CENTRE FOR BRISTOL DEVELOPMENT CORPORATION 1993

Architecture Today September 1992

Thom Gorst, *The Buildings Around Us*, 1993

Robert Kronenburg, *Portable Architecture*, 1993

Neil Parkyn, *Local Heroes, ABC&D*, February 1993

Samantha Hardingham, *England – a guide to recent architecture*,1995

Tony Aldous, *C20/21 Bristol's Modern Buildings*, 2000

- RIBA Award
- Institute of Structural Engineers Award
- British Construction Industry Award

ST. ANNE'S COLLEGE, OXFORD 1992

Architects Journal 11 August 1993

Samantha Hardingham, *England – a guide to recent architecture*,1995

English Heritage, *Shared Interest*, 2007

- RIBA Award

REDCLIFF QUAY, BRISTOL 1991

Neil Parkyn, *Local Heroes, ABC&D*, February 1993

Tony Aldous, *C20/21 Bristol's Modern Buildings*, 2000

Andrew Foyle, Pevsner Architectural Guides, *Bristol*, 2004

- Bristol Civic Society Award

31 GREAT GEORGE STREET, BRISTOL 1990

Neil Parkyn, *Local Heroes, ABC&D*, February 1993

Tony Aldous, *C20/21 Bristol's Modern Buildings*, 2000

Andrew Foyle, Pevsner Architectural Guides, *Bristol*, 2004

- Bristol Civic Society Award

KING EDWARD'S JUNIOR SCHOOL, BATH 1990

Michael Forsyth, Pevsner Architectural Guides, *Bath*, 2003

- RIBA Award

SOUTHGATE STREET, BATH 1989

Architects Journal 9 November 1988

ONE BRIDEWELL STREET, BRISTOL 1987

BRE Energy Efficiency in Offices, Good Practice Study, May 1991

Neil Parkyn, *Local Heroes, ABC&D*, February 1993

Tony Aldous, *C20/21 Bristol's Modern Buildings*, 2000

Andrew Foyle, Pevsner Architectural Guides, *Bristol*, 2004

- RIBA Award

SALVATION ARMY CITADEL, BRISTOL 1987

- Civic Trust Award

ST. MARY'S CENTRE, THORNBURY 1983

- Civic Trust Commendation

OLD MARKET CENTRE, TAUNTON 1982

- Civic Trust Commendation

78-100 ST MICHAEL'S HILL, HOUSING, BRISTOL 1980

- Europa Nostra Diploma of Merit

MEMBERS OF THE PRACTICE 1980-2010

Adrian Jones
Alan Quick
Alex Legge
Alison Bromilow
Alistair Brierley
Alistair Green
Andrew Brown
Andrew Lolley
Andy Cotton
Annegret Thiede

Barbara Hicks
Bill Jacques
Bob Drew
Brandon Lloyd
Brenda Taylor
Brian Sprake

Carina Richards
Carol Carey
Caroline Pitt
Charles Gregory
Chris Colyer
Chris Mitchell

Danusia Lewis
David Hackett
David Kent
David Mellor
David Ricks
David Tyrer
Derek Robinson
Diana Bush
Diane Gitsham
Dominic Leaver
Don Nicholson

Ed Harris
Ed Tharby
Elspeth Faulkner
Esme Pavelin

Frances Streipert

Gayle Stevens
Geoff Crozier
Geoff Davis
George McManus
Gina Hunt
Glen Gareis
Glenn Moses
Graham Preston
Graham Scott-Robertson

Helen Brunskill
Helen Finnemore
Helen Hollis
Helen Lawrence
Helen Safe
Helena Durrant
Henry Alpass
Hilda Chagula
Huw James

Ian Smith
Ian Stevenson
Ian Thornton

Jan Lenz
Jane Ferneyhough
Jenny Gossage
Jeremy Dane
John Fjeld
John Franklin
John Harrison
John Hartnell
John Tidman
Jon Chadwick
Jon Lorth
Jonathan Davey
Joy Clarke
Joy Stone
Judith Hoskin
Juli Rolls
Justin Leadbetter

Karlene Williams
Kasia Freyer
Keith Boxer

Laurence Smith
Les Constable
Linda Appleton
Linda McManus
Liz Davis
Louise Ciotti
Lynsey Lucas
Lynsey Smith
Lynton Pepper

Mac Gay
Mark Baylis
Mark Osborne
Martin Begbie
Martin Gibson
Mary Mulcahy
Matt Harrison
Maurice King

Michael Collings
Mike Speechly

Neil Stacey
Niall Bird
Nick Eager
Nick Stubbs
Nick Vaughan
Nicola Harvey
Nicole Hansmeier
Nigel Dyke
Nigel Honer
Nigel Rayner
Nigel Widdup

Oliver Grimshaw
Oliver Smith

Paul Appleton
Paul Kobbe
Paul Maddox
Penny Mellor
Peter Ashby
Peter Lankester
Peter Meacock
Peter Tay
Peter Thompson
Phillip Yunnie

Rachel Scott
Ray Lambe
Raymond Down
Raynor Nixon
Richard Lavington
Richard Lee
Richard Silverman
Robert Allen
Robert Melvin
Robert Mills
Robert Wilton
Robin Gray
Roden Buxton
Roger Foster
Roger Guck
Roger Stephens
Ron Jupp
Ruth Nielsen

Sharon Fennell
Shaun Griffiths
Siew Cheong
Simon Dlugiewicz
Simon Hatcher
Simon Lawrence

Simon Rayner
Spencer Back
Steve Hynds
Steve Parrock

Tamsin Thomas
Ted Nash
Ted Pitcher
Tim Burgess
Tim Crosskey
Tim Must
Tobias Feilding-Crawley
Toby Jefferies
Tom Bomford
Tom Russell
Tony Currivan

Vera Forsyth
Vicky Browne

Zac Nicholson

Photographers

Roger Ball
Peter Cook
Simon Doling
Fotohaus
Mary Lowance
Lance McNulty
Stephen Morris
Alison Needler
Neil Porter
William Pye
Paul Riddle
Nathan Sale
Steve Townsend
John Trelawny Ross
Adam Wilson
Charlotte Wood

Every effort has been made to acknowledge
the photographers we have used. We
apologise for any omissions.